COWBOY COOKING

Recipes from the Cowboy Artists of America®

INTRODUCTION BY
JANE JUSTIN

COMPILED AND EDITED BY
THOMAS M. WATSON
Secretary-Treasurer, Business Manager,
Honorary Member, Historian,
and sometimes trail-ride cook

Northland Publishing

The first edition of this book was entitled *His Friends' Cookbook: Favorite Foods and Trail Ride Fun of the Cowboy Artists of America*, published in 1986 by the CAA. This revised edition is produced by agreement and with permission of the CAA.

Cover Design by David Jenney
Book Design by Carolyn Gibbs

Manufactured in the United States of America

Cover: *Too Many Biscuits* © 1986 by James Boren
Copyright © 1991 by COWBOY ARTISTS OF AMERICA
All rights reserved.

FIRST EDITION, REVISED
Second printing, 1992
Third printing, 1993
Fourth printing, 1995
ISBN 0-87358-528-3

Library of Congress Catalog Card Number 91-50741

0574/7.5M/6-95

CONTENTS

FOREWORD

IN LATE 1975, it was decided that CAA should do a cookbook and that I, as Business Manager, could compile and edit it. But time, trouble, and ignorance caused delays. From time to time, others contacted CAA about doing a cookbook, but, for one reason or another, it never got "done." Eventually time and trouble passed, and I got back into the "fire."

Cooking is a lot like courting. At first, appearance is quite important. But once you have experienced the pleasure of a good dish, appearance matters less. Later it is oftentimes possible to experiment with shortcuts that will produce equally pleasing results. Sometimes it's possible to add touches of your own that make it even better. That's why the "art" of cooking should never be "stale," but ever-growing. So test and experiment; explore new recipes. Otherwise, why buy another cookbook?

It is said that the first cookbook was produced in Sicily in the fifth century B.C. According to *Women's Book of World Records and Achievements,* Fannie Farmer, who wrote the *Boston Cooking School Cook Book,* published in 1896, is credited with being the first to give "explicit directions and level measurements" in recipes. With her instructions, each cook could produce relatively the same dish.

At times, you may think this book is a throwback to pre-Fannie Farmer days. Some cooks just don't understand that: a dash is not a marathon, a pinch is not a grab and a sprinkle is not a downpour. An artist once told me that every horse he painted he had either seen, ridden or made-up. Well, every recipe in this book I have either seen, eaten or made-up.

Throughout this book, I have scattered Hints, Observations, Guides and Sayings (HOGS), which are identified with a hog symbol. Here's the first.

Of course you knew that one. Enjoy! But don't expect a chefs-d'oeuvre.

Read a recipe all the way through before you start preparing it.

ACKNOWLEDGMENTS

OF COURSE I THANK the Cowboy Artists of America family; the Active, Emeritus and Honorary members, past and present, and their spouses. A special thanks to Toni, my wife, who did a lot of typing and who prepared many of the recipes for me to try. Another, to Mary Margaret Sams, my secretary, who also did an awful lot of typing. Thanks to "Mother" Jane Justin, Evelyn Herman, Pat Finney, Ramon Hartnett, Barney Nelson, Lewis Smith and the Reference Department of the Kansas City Public Library for their help and contributions.

It has been suggested that some prehistoric man probably happened upon the charred carcass of an unfortunate animal that had been unable to escape a lightning-ignited grass or forest fire. Upon touching the hot meat, that person jerked burned fingers back and stuck them in his mouth to relieve the pain, thus sampling the first cooked food. I thank that prehistoric person and all cooks and chefs who have since elaborated upon and added to that original dish.

I've corrected some mistakes: "jushrooms," "farlic," "uncivered," "rasins," "vinella," "Worchestershire," "thinkly," (thinly or thickly) and "mix in a small bowel" (bowl). All remaining errors are mine.

INTRODUCTION

FLAVORS OF THE WEST come through in food as well as they do in the works of the talented CAA members. You'll find that's true as you try the recipes in this book. When you use one of Sharon Beeler's recipes, you may feel you know a little more about Joe and his work.

More people today—no matter what their income—are doing their own cooking. Men and women alike are searching out and embellishing upon interesting and unusual recipes that make cooking a creative art, not a chore. When you plan a meal, cook the food and set a beautiful table for your family or friends; you have an artistic creation such as any on an artist's easel. You have produced another "art form."

This is one reason I think this book is so appropriate. A "work of art" from the kitchen can be doubly enjoyable, through both the eye and the mouth. Tom Watson has worked long and hard to compile this book and I know his hope is that you will use it and create many "artistic" meals.

JANE JUSTIN
Fort Worth, Texas

ACTIVE MEMBERS

SHARON'S SEDONA SALAD

4   cups greens (romaine, spinach, lettuce, etc.) torn
1   large tomato, sliced
1   small green pepper, sliced
1   small onion, sliced and separated into rings
1   tsp oregano
6   radishes, sliced
8   black olives, sliced

4   anchovy fillets, optional
6   Tbs olive oil
2   Tbs lemon juice or wine vinegar
    Salt and ground black pepper to taste
1   medium cucumber, sliced
1/4 cup crumbled Feta cheese

Combine and toss. Serves 4-6.

INDIAN SPINACH SALAD

DRESSING:
1/4   cup white wine vinegar
1/4   cup salad oil
2   Tbs chopped chutney
2   Tbs apple juice concentrate
1 1/2 tsp curry powder
1   tsp dry mustard

SALAD:
      Torn spinach
1 1/2 cups diced apple
1/2   cup raisins
1/2   cup nuts
1/3   cup sunflower seeds
3   Tbs chopped green onions

Mix dressing. Mix salad, add dressing and toss. Serves 4-6.

SPINACH FANDANGO

1   lb lean ground beef
1   medium onion, chopped
1   can (7 oz) button mushrooms
1-2   cloves garlic, chopped and pressed
1   tsp oregano
1/3   cup salad oil
      Salt & pepper to taste

2   12-oz pkgs frozen chopped spinach
1   can (10 1/2 ozs) cream of celery soup
1   cup sour cream
2   large slices mozzarella or jack cheese, cut into strips

Put oil in large skillet, add meat, onion, mushrooms, garlic and oregano. Brown, stirring frequently. Salt and pepper to taste. Place frozen spinach on top of other ingredients, cover and let steam until spinach is cooked. Blend. Pour mixture from skillet into a medium sized casserole dish. Blend celery soup and sour cream and stir into meat mixture. Garnish with cheese strips. Bake at 350°, uncovered, for 15-20 minutes. Serves 6-8.

The oil can be varied, depending on how rich you want it. Also, I often add a small amount of uncooked minute rice or noodles to absorb some of the moisture from the frozen spinach.

CORN ON THE COB

Ears of corn	1 **Tbs sugar per gal of water**
Water to cover	1 **Tbs lemon juice per gal of water**

At least one hour before cooking, remove all the silk and the outer husks from the corn (leave some of the husks on). Then plunge the corn into snow-cold water (use ice cubes if necessary). At cooking time put the corn into the water, add sugar and lemon juice. Bring to boil and cook for one or two minutes, depending on size and age of corn. Remove from heat and let stand for at least ten minutes or until ready to serve. If necessary, corn may be reheated, quickly, just to boiling, not a second longer, then served immediately. Makes as much as you want.

MEXICAN CHICKEN

1	**whole chicken**	1	**can chili salsa**
	Water to cover	1	**can diced green chilies**
	Cumin	1	**stick butter**
	Salt & pepper to taste	12	**corn tortillas, cut up**
1	**can cream of mushroom soup**	1	**medium onion, diced**
1	**can cream of chicken soup**		

Boil chicken, cumin, salt and pepper together until cooked. Cool and bone. Cut into slices and/or bite-sized pieces. Combine soups, salsa and chilies. Heat. Cook onions in butter, then add pieces of tortillas and continue cooking until butter is absorbed. In a casserole dish, layer tortilla mixture, then chicken, and cover with sauce. May be topped with grated cheese. Bake at 350° for 20-30 minutes. Serves 4-6.

For uncooked dishes, add the herbs as soon as possible and let stand in the refrigerator overnight if possible. For slow or long cooking dishes add the herbs the last twenty or thirty minutes.

YUM KAAX BUTTER SAUCE

$^1/_2$ **cup (1 stick) butter or margarine, melted**	1	**Tbs lemon juice**
	1	**tsp chili powder**

Mix ingredients well. Keep hot over a candle or on a heated tray. Apply with a brush.

INCA BUTTER

1	cup (2 sticks) butter or margarine, soft
1/2	tsp dry mustard
1	Tbs chopped chives
1/2	tsp curry powder, best quality
1/8	tsp cayenne pepper
	Salt to taste

Combine the above and mix well.

Sift dry ingredients after combining to mix thoroughly.

Herb Butter: Blend together 1 stick of unsalted butter or margarine, 1-2 tablespoonfuls dried herbs or herb blend (double the amount if fresh herbs are used) and 1/2 teaspoon lemon juice.

CHOCOLATE CAKE

2	cups sugar	1	cup water
2	cups flour	1/2	cup buttermilk
1	stick margarine	2	eggs, slightly beaten
1/2	cup Crisco	1	tsp soda
4	Tbs cocoa	1	tsp vanilla

Sift sugar and flour together into a large bowl. Put margarine, Crisco, cocoa and water into a saucepan, bring to a rapid boil and pour over flour and sugar mixture. Mix well. Add remaining ingredients, mix well. Pour into greased 16-by-1-inch jelly roll pan and bake at 400° for 20-25 minutes.

ICING

Start icing five minutes before cake finishes baking.

1	stick margarine	1	box powdered sugar
4	Tbs cocoa	1	tsp vanilla
1/3	cup milk	1	cup walnuts or pecans, chopped

Melt margarine in saucepan, add cocoa and milk. Bring to a boil and remove from heat. Add other ingredients. Beat well and spread on cake while it is still in pan and hot.

CAA TRAIL RIDE

THE MAIN PURPOSE of the trail ride is to familiarize the members with different areas of the American West and to afford them the opportunity to research by experience and/or to observe various cowboy skills, work and everyday situations. Also, it furthers the acquaintance, camaraderie and cooperation of the members, one with the other, and every effort is made to promote these purposes.

On every ride business meetings are held and "tip sheets" for the Limited Edition Catalog are signed by all the artists.

The year 1967 was really more of an artist gathering than a CAA trail ride. Most of the artists were CAA members, but others were also present: Ginger Renner, Olaf Wieghorst and Wolfgang Pogzeba; wives and children attended too. Almost everyone stayed at a campgrounds half-a-mile east of the Jackson, Wyoming, city square. They used tents, trailer houses, and motels. No one went horseback riding. There were reports of gun shots during the night.

THE FIRST ACTUAL COWBOY ARTISTS OF AMERICA trail ride was in 1968 on the Slash Ranch south of Old Horse Springs, New Mexico. Host Bob Lee had been an Associate member; CAA's Associate membership status was voted out earlier that year. The Lees use both the S Lazy S and the VIN brands. Five CAA members were on that ride. Everyone was responsible for his own food and sleeping arrangements. They did quite a bit of horseback riding. There was also lots of target practice. Hampton won the last go-round with a hip shot. It rained.

CAA'S 1969 TRAIL RIDE was on Richard Harris' Seven Lazy H Bar Ranch, just north of Pagosa Springs, Colorado. There were a number of firsts on that ride: the CAA trail ride buckle was worn; some members learned that George Marks snored; Fred Fellows gave a demonstration of trick and fancy roping. Nonmember guests were invited; I was the guest of Byron Wolfe.

I took along some Dr. Pepper. Gordon Snidow drank one and asked if I went to the toilet a lot, adding, "This stuff is nothing but prune juice." Since then I have made an issue of having Dr. Pepper on each trail ride.

In a lineshack kitchen, Marks, Snidow and I fried potatoes and onions, fixed corn-on-the-cob, cornbread and cake. Outside, Fred Fellows, Chuck King and Mr. Harris built a fire to grill steaks. The wood was wet so they used Coleman fuel to ignite it. A trail of fuel was dribbled from the fireplace to the fuel can. When they lit the fire, it immediately spread to the fuel can, which was right next to Fellows. People inside the lineshack could see what was happening almost before Fred did. Some yelled instructions and ran to his aid; some just yelled. Fred calmly picked up a big sack of ripe peaches and "squashed" out the fire. For a while we called him "Peaches," but we don't do that anymore.

One day Joe Beeler's horse reared backwards and fell. Joe jumped clear of the horse, but in the process punched four holes in the top of his left knee with his own spur. There was no doctor on the ride so Joe was taken to town for a tetanus shot.

Byron Wolfe was not a big man and was generally given a smaller horse. Once he lagged about 100 yards behind everyone else. The whole group stopped, but didn't want him to feel they were waiting for him. As a ruse, Bill Moyers got off his horse, removed the saddle, adjusted the blanket and then re-saddled. When Byron got within ear-shot, many of the guys began lecturing Moyers on how to saddle-up, chiding him that had it been done properly the first time, it wouldn't have been necessary for everyone to stop while he made adjustments. I don't believe Byron ever knew why they really stopped and waited.

Byron also had taken along a new leather belt for everyone to sign. When he got it back, it had twenty-one names on it; the names of the nineteen men on the trail ride, plus C.M. Russell and Frederic Remington. Byron thought it had been done by S.O.B., Snidow or Beeler. Riding home he kept pressing me about who'd done it. Finally, I asked, "Of the nineteen men on the ride, who would be the last one you'd suspect?"

He answered, "Tom Ryan."

"I rest my case," I replied.

Again it rained, but that's another whole story.

IN 1970, CAA WENT TO STANLEY WILLIAMSON'S ranch near Blanco, Texas. We were on the sheep-and- goat portion of the Circle W with no cattle to rope, so we went out and roped armadillos.

Again, each person was responsible for his own meals and bedding. Byron Wolfe and I rented a fold-out camping trailer. We invited George Marks and Gordon Snidow, both good cooks, to use the extra bunks; that's when the rest of us learned George snored. We couldn't wake up George and no one else could get to sleep. About 4 A.M. Byron said, "If anyone can pray, pray for dawn. " One morning one of the guests wouldn't get up, so they stood him up in his "mummy" sleeping bag and proceeded to see how much water it would hold.

Charlie Schreiner III furnished some "gentle" mounts; one of them threw Charlie himself. Joe Beeler gave a demonstration in both shooting and night vision.

When members gathered for the business meeting, President Snidow pulled a Colt 45, fired it into the air and said, "This meeting will come to order."

At the host's dinner, the main meat dish was "cabritto," a first for many.

Jim Reynolds sprained his ankle and had to visit a local doctor; again there wasn't a doctor on the ride.

DINING OUT

RIB ROAST IN ROCK SALT CRUST
(Western Style)

10	**lbs standing rib roast**	**¹/₂**	**cup water**
3	**cups rock salt**		**Covered roasting pan**

Let the rib roast stand at room temperature at least 8 hours. Place rock salt in a bowl, moisten with the water.

Place roast, rib side down, in a large roasting pan. Pack the moistened rock salt over the top and sides of the roast. Cover roaster and place in preheated 500° oven for one hour. Reduce temperature to 350° for one hour more; then turn oven off, allowing roast to remain in the oven for another hour. Do not open your roaster at any time during the 3 hours. Remove from oven and allow to cool 15-20 minutes. Crack off salt, slice roast and serve. Roast will be done on the outside and rare to medium rare on the inside.

FRUITED BUFFALO POT ROAST

12	dried apricots	¹/₄	tsp ginger
12	dried prunes	3	whole cloves
3-4	lbs buffalo roast	1	medium onion, sliced
1	cup cider or apple juice		Water, shortening, salt and
2	Tbs sugar		pepper to taste
¹/₄	tsp cinnamon		

Cover apricots and prunes with water. Soak several hours. Meanwhile, brown roast on all sides in a little hot fat; season with salt and pepper. Combine cider, sugar, cinnamon, ginger and cloves; pour over meat. Add onions. Cover; simmer 2 hours or until meat is almost tender. Drain fruits; place atop meat and cook 30 minutes longer. Thicken liquid in pan for gravy. Beef chuck roast may be used if you have a shortage of buffalo!

HASSENFEFFER

1	cup red wine
¹/₂	cup vinegar
1	cup water
2	tsp salt
¹/₄	tsp pepper
¹/₂	tsp whole cloves
2	tsp sugar
4	bay leaves
1	medium onion, sliced
1	rabbit, about 2¹/₂ lbs, cut into serving pieces
3	Tbs fat
2	tsp Worcestershire sauce
3	Tbs flour

Mix first nine ingredients (liquids, spices, seasonings and onion) in a glass or enamelware bowl. Place rabbit and sliced giblets in mixture and marinate for 8 to 10 hours in refrigerator, turning occasionally. Save liquid and onion, discard bay leaves and cloves. Remove meat, pat dry and roll in flour; brown on all sides in hot fat in large skillet. Pour marinade over rabbit, cover and cook over low heat for 1 hour, or until tender. Remove rabbit. Add Worcestershire to skillet. Mix flour with a little cold water to make a paste, then add a few tablespoonfuls of hot liquid to the paste, mix well, and pour into skillet; stir until smooth and thick. Pour over rabbit. Serves 4-6.

Peel onions without tears!

I've heard of several methods; the last two work best for me:

1

Point the root-end down, don't cut the roots off, work with the onion in that position.

2

Hold a wooden "kitchen match" between your teeth and lips.

3

Hold a piece of white bread between your teeth and lips.

4

Cut the onion in half and rub both cut edges with a lemon wedge.

5

Peel the onion while it is submerged in water.

6

First, store the onion in the refrigerator overnight.

7

Hold the onion close to an open flame while working with it (gas stove flame or lighted candles work). CAUTION!

BLANQUETTE de POULET

2 cans chicken broth

5 carrots, scraped and quartered

1 lb tiny white onions, peeled

$^{1}/_{2}$ cup thinly sliced celery

$^{1}/_{2}$ lb mushrooms, sliced

2 cups quick-cooking brown rice

Vegetable broth powder to taste

2 whole boneless, skinless chicken
breasts, cut in 1" cubes

2 Tbs cornstarch

2 Tbs lemon juice

I use two large saucepans and one large skillet. Put $^{1}/_{2}$ cup chicken broth, carrots, onions and celery into one pan and simmer for 20 minutes; add mushrooms and simmer 10 minutes more. In other pan prepare rice per instructions on package, season with vegetable broth powder and keep warm. Put chicken and remainder of broth in skillet and gently simmer for 30 minutes. With a slotted spoon, move the chicken to the vegetable mixture in the first pan; keep warm. Pour broth from skillet and save. Mix a little broth and cornstarch in skillet and stir until smooth. Stirring constantly, gradually add remainder of the broth and, continuing to stir, bring to boil; then simmer until thickened. Stir in lemon juice. Stir sauce into chicken and vegetable mixture. Serve over rice. Serves 6.

EASTER-EGG BREAD

1	cup warm water	2	pkgs yeast
1½	cups sifted all-purpose flour	¾	cup shortening
1	cup sugar	1½	tsp salt
2	eggs	1	egg, separated
2	Tbs lemon juice	3¼	cups sifted all-purpose flour
6-8	eggs, colored but not cooked	1	Tbs cream
	Rainbow nonpareils, to sprinkle		

Pour water into a large mixing bowl, sprinkle yeast over water and stir until dissolved. Add 1½ cups flour all at once; stir until smooth. Cover bowl with cloth and let stand in warm place (85°-90°) for 1½ hours. With electric mixer on medium, beat shortening until creamy; gradually add sugar and salt, beating all the time, mix thoroughly. Beat in 2 eggs and one egg white until smooth and fluffy. Stir in lemon juice and yeast mixture. Add enough flour to make dough that can be handled easily; place dough in large greased bowl. Brush dough with melted shortening. Cover bowl with cloth and let dough rise until doubled in bulk. Turn dough onto floured board; knead gently and let rest for two minutes. Divide dough in half; form into two ropes about 36 inches long. Grease large cookie sheet; take ropes and form a loosely braided ring, leaving gaps for the colored eggs—insert eggs. Let dough rise until almost doubled in bulk. Bake at 350° for 10 minutes. Beat egg yolk and cream together, brush on bread; sprinkle on nonpareils. Bake 30-40 minutes more, or until done. Colored eggs will be hard-cooked.

HOT POTATO SALAD

4	lbs small white or pink potatoes	½	tsp garlic salt
1	lb sliced lean bacon	¼	tsp ground pepper
2	lbs frankfurters, thinly sliced at an angle	⅔	cup vinegar
		⅔	cup water
1½	cups red onions, chopped	4	scallions or green onions, chopped
3	tsp flour		
2	Tbs sugar	1	dozen eggs, hard-boiled, sliced
3	tsp salt		Fresh parsley, chopped

Boil potatoes, covered, for 30-35 minutes, just until tender. Meanwhile, sauté bacon until crisp; remove to paper towel. In bacon fat, sauté frankfurter slices until brown, turning frequently. Remove franks with slotted spoon and keep warm. Remove all but about four tablespoons of the bacon fat; in this, sauté one cup of red onions until soft. Mix together flour, sugar, salts and pepper; slowly blend in the water and vinegar mixture. Stir into sautéed onion and simmer until thickened, stirring frequently. Peel potatoes, slice (not too thick), and add to dressing. Remove from heat and add the remaining raw onions and scallions; toss with potatoes and dressing. Into large salad bowl arrange layers of potato salad, frankfurters, egg slices and crumbled bacon, ending with bacon on top. Sprinkle with parsley. Serves 12, or Harvey and Tom.

PAPER BAG APPLE PIE

1	9-inch pastry shell, unbaked	$^1/_4$	tsp ground cloves
6	medium green apples	2	Tbs lemon juice
$^1/_2$	cup brown sugar (for filling)	$^1/_2$	cup brown sugar (for topping)
2	Tbs flour (for filling)	$^1/_2$	cup flour (for topping)
$^1/_4$	tsp cinnamon	$^1/_2$	cup (1 stick) margarine

Pare, core and slice apples into large bowl. Combine the spices in a small bowl, add the filling sugar and flour, mix; sprinkle over apples. Toss apples to coat well; then spoon into pastry shell and drizzle with lemon juice. Combine topping sugar and flour in a small bowl, cut in margarine until well mixed. Sprinkle over apples to cover top. Slide pie into a moist, heavy brown paper bag, large enough to cover pie loosely. Fold open end over twice and fasten with paper clips or staples. Mist paper bag occasionally to prevent fire. Place on large cookie sheet and bake at 425° for one hour. Split bag open, remove pie, cool on a wire rack.

FRUIT AND NUT BARS

1	lb pkg frozen black sweet cherries, pitted and without sugar	2	tsp baking powder
$1^1/_2$	cups unbleached, pre-sifted flour	4	eggs, slightly beaten
$1^1/_2$	cups brown or white sugar	1	tsp vanilla
1	tsp salt	2	cups unsalted cashew pieces

Partially defrost cherries in package, then chop and place in sieve to drain and finish thawing. Stir flour, sugar, salt and baking powder together in a large bowl. Add eggs, vanilla, fruit and nuts. Mix well and spread thinly on ungreased teflon cookie pan with sides. Bake at 350° for 13 minutes. Reduce heat to 325° for 12 minutes. Cool, cut into bars and sprinkle with confectioner's sugar if desired. Dates and walnuts may be substituted for cherries and cashews.

WHEN THE BOYS WERE SMALL, we drove to Quebec and, inevitably, found ourselves in an attractive French restaurant. The four male members of the family watched as I perused the menu; supposedly, I knew some French, and they awaited my suggestion. Then I saw "Foie de Veau" and ordered. When the waiter set five plates of steaming calves' liver before us, four shocked, accusing faces turned to the traitor in their midst. I thought I'd ordered veal. When Harvey got his voice back, he told the boys they needn't eat the liver, just the vegetables; small consolation. I avoided catching anyone's eye as I savored every bite of delicious liver. The evening was saved by fabulous French desserts.

Always start with eggs at room temperature.

CAA TRAIL RIDE

FRED FELLOWS AND JIM REYNOLDS got a chuck wagon to use in 1971. CA rode on the IX Ranch, operated by Art and Audrey Roth, north of Big Sandy, Montana. I was asked to cook for everyone and agreed to do so if Joe Beeler would be the fireman. We were supposed to fix two meals a day, no lunch. Day one, we had breakfast and were on the trail before eight A.M., back in camp by noon. Everyone wanted lunch. So, we got out tuna, boiled eggs, diced pickles, chopped onions, mixed in pickle juice and mayonnaise and poured in the peas. (I'd always put in peas so the kids would get a vegetable.) Some riders had tuna salad; others made tuna sandwiches.

I'd heard of beer pancakes, so for one breakfast I decided to make bourbon pancakes; mixed them up with Jack Daniels. The batter was beautiful and fluffy, it smelled great. When John Hampton wanted seconds, he held out his plate and said, "Pour me another one."

Although we fried steaks and made beef stew, pineapple upside-down cake, John Wayne's Favorite Casserole and other unique dishes, Fred once told someone the menu consisted of Dr. Pepper and pea sandwiches. The minutes of the membership meeting read, "The meeting was adjourned for a beer and a Dr. Pepper."

Hampton killed a rattlesnake, skinned it and applied the skin, as trim, to the cantle of his saddle, as in a Russell painting; that was Russell Country. Then the stories turned to snakes, how they mate and how mates look for each other at dusk. I don't think John really believed the stories, but when he went to sleep in his tent, the saddle was out in the field, fifty yards away.

Someone found a bleached bovine shoulder bone with a buffalo skull drawn on it and the initials C.M.R. But nobody was taken in—the ink was hardly dry. However, a "seed" had been planted.

It was so hot the flies on the spiral fly paper above the chuck wagon table slid slowly down to the bottom. I was accused of serving rice and raisins; I hadn't even taken any raisins along. And it was windy—so windy that to play poker everyone had to have a rock to hold his cards down. The dealer had to push cards under the rocks; the penalty for a misdeal was to match the pot. That was a rule Frank Polk didn't like.

Snidow waded out into a foot-deep creek. He started digging, throwing the mud downstream and soon he had a clear, cool, deep bathing hole.

Bob Scriver, who lived at Browning, brought his own horse on the ride.

No one got hurt, as we now had a doctor along and have had one ever since.

CHILI VERDE

2 **lbs lean stew meat, cut in chunks**	3 **cans Ortega green chilies**
1/2 **small onion, chopped**	**Good-sized tomato, cut up**
1 **clove garlic, minced**	**(optional)**
1 **tsp oregano**	**Salt to taste**

Use a large skillet, about three quarts. Put onion and garlic on the bottom, place meat chunks on top, place pan on heat. The meat will start to steam, but eventually the liquid will evaporate and the meat will begin to brown. When well browned, add chilies, oregano and salt. Fill pan with water and boil until chilies fall apart; more water may be added. Add the tomato toward the last, optional. Cook until meat is done and you have the desired juice level. Serve hot with buttered, fresh flour tortillas. Serves 4-6. I usually make a large batch so we can have some later. It's almost better the next day. Freezes well too.

CHEESECAKE

1 1/2 **cups graham cracker crumbs, or**	3/4 **cup plus 2 Tbs sugar**
20 single crackers crumbled	2 **tsp vanilla**
3 **Tbs sugar**	1/4 **tsp salt**
1 1/2 **tsp cinnamon**	1 **tsp fresh lemon juice**
1/3 **cup butter, melted**	2 **cups sour cream**
1 **16-oz pkg cream cheese, softened**	4 **Tbs sugar**
2 **eggs, well beaten**	2 **tsp vanilla**

U G Speed

Thoroughly mix the first four ingredients. Spread this mixture over the bottom of a 9-x-9-inch glass, oven-proof dish. Freeze overnight. Next day, combine the next six ingredients and mix until creamed. Pour this mixture over the frozen crust and bake at 350° for 18 minutes. Meanwhile, mix the sour cream, remaining sugar and vanilla. Remove the cake from the oven, pour the second mixture over the baked mixture and return it to the oven to bake 5 more minutes. Chill several hours. Serve with warm Cherry Topping.

CHERRY TOPPING

$3/4$ cup sugar
1 Tbs flour
1 egg, beaten

1 can pie cherries and juice
Red food coloring, few drops

Combine the above ingredients and cook down to desired thickness.

HOT DIP

1 lb lean ground beef
$1/2$ onion, minced
1 clove garlic, minced
$6^1/2$-8 oz can of jalapeno bean dip
1 can refried beans

$1/2$ bottle green enchilada sauce, mild
$1/2$ lb Velveeta cheese, sliced
$1/4$ tsp ground cumin, or less

Fry the meat, onion and garlic together. Mix in the dip, beans, sauce and cumin. Lay cheese slices on top and melt. Serve hot with tortilla chips or roll it up in hot floured tortillas. Looks aren't everything.

Many people believe the outdoors improves the taste of food. Mark Twain said, "Nothing helps scenery like ham and eggs."

CHOCOLATE SAUCE

2 cups sugar
1 cup water
$1/2$ cup cocoa

1 can Eagle Brand sweetened condensed milk

Use a large, heavy pan, because this boils up! Mix first three ingredients and boil, without stirring, for 6 minutes. Remove from heat and add the condensed milk; mix. Great on ice cream; delicious by itself. Satisfies my sweet tooth and can cheer me up on a gloomy day. Excellent with fresh strawberries.

VANILLA ICE CREAM

4	eggs	6	cups light cream
2¹/₂	cups sugar	2	Tbs vanilla
4	cups milk	¹/₂	tsp salt

Beat eggs until light. Add sugar gradually, beating at fast speed until mixture thickens. Add remaining ingredients; mix thoroughly. Freeze in ice cream freezer according to directions. Makes 1 gallon. Serve with chocolate sauce.

PULL & TUCK ROLLS

18-20	frozen rolls	¹/₂	cup brown sugar
¹/₂	pkg instant butterscotch pudding, dry	1	tsp cinnamon
			Nuts & raisins to taste
1	stick butter, melted		

Put rolls in greased bundt pan. Pour other ingredients, in order, over the rolls; cover with Saran wrap and let rise 8 hours, or overnight for breakfast rolls. Bake at 350° for 25 minutes. Turn upside down on plate; the syrup runs all over the rolls. Pull them apart and tuck them away.

CUCUMBERS IN SOUR CREAM

2	cucumbers, peel & slice	2	Tbs chopped dill pickles & juice
1	Tbs salt	¹/₄	tsp sugar
1	cup sour cream		Pepper & parsley to taste
2	Tbs lemon juice		Cold water to cover cucumbers
¹/₂	tsp salt		

Cover sliced cucumbers with cold water and 1 tablespoon salt. Combine all other ingredients. Drain cucumbers and add to mixture; mix. Serves 2-4.

CRAB IMPOSSIBLE PIE

4	cups grated cheddar cheese	1	cup Bisquick
1	lb imitation crab meat	2	Tbs chopped green onions
4	eggs		Hollandaise sauce
2	cups milk		

Put cheese into a 7-x-11-inch glass dish, cover with crab meat. Combine eggs, milk and Bisquick. Add onion, mix well. Pour over cheese and crab meat. Bake at 400° for 40-45 minutes. Serve with hollandaise sauce.

CAA TRAIL RIDE

BY 1972, EVERYONE HAD HAD ENOUGH of worrying about preparing trail ride meals; we've had outside cooks ever since.

John Justin and Paul Weaver were hosts that year. They served mountain oyster hors d'oeuvres and lots of giant T-bone steaks. The ride was through Ponderosa pine on the Mogollon Rim in Arizona, on Ernest Chisholm's Bar T Bar Ranch near Flagstaff.

Fritz White rode horseback for the first time in his life. During the morning break, he didn't even get off his horse—afraid he wouldn't be able to get back on. Once, his mare stepped on a section of metal that flipped up and caught in the back cinch; several people ran to the mare's aid, before Fritz could "buck 'er out."

We had our first almost all-night penny-ante poker game.

Fred Fellows and Bud Helbig drove from Montana in an R.V. En route they lost a rope can and a pair of new boots off the top of the vehicle; the can contained ropes and $200. They said that going home, they'd watch for someone spinning a rope, wearing new boots and sporting a $200 smile.

Fred brought a roping dummy; it was in continuous use.

Brownell McGrew came on that ride; he brought his own horse, a small, grey Arabian mare. And *Western Horseman* publisher Dick Spencer was there, too. More rain; ranchers were beginning to like having CAA on their place.

CALABACITAS CON CARNE

$1^1/_2$ lbs round steak, or sirloin, cubed
4   Tbs shortening
$^1/_2$ cup water
5   medium zucchini squash, diced
1   medium onion, sliced and
     separated into rings

2   cups white corn kernels, drained
$^1/_2$ cup chopped green chilies
2   tsp garlic salt
1   tsp salt
1   cup cheddar cheese, grated

Brown meat in 2 tablespoons shortening. Reduce heat, add water, cover and simmer until tender, about one hour. Add more water if necessary. Sauté squash and onion rings in 2 tablespoons shortening until slightly tender, about ten minutes. Add corn, chilies and seasonings. Add meat and meat stock to vegetables, simmer about twenty minutes to blend flavors. Add grated cheese and stir well. Serves 8.

WM·MOYERS

TEXAS CAKE

2 cups flour	3 sticks margarine
2 cups sugar	8 Tbs Hershey cocoa
2 eggs	5 Tbs milk
1 tsp baking soda	2 cups powdered sugar, sifted
1/2 tsp salt	1 tsp vanilla
1/2 cup sour cream	1 cup chopped pecans
1 cup water	

Mix flour, sugar, eggs, baking soda, salt and sour cream. Mix water, 2 sticks margarine and 5 tablespoons cocoa and bring to a boil. Combine the two mixtures. Pour into greased pan (15-x-10-x-2-inch). Bake at 350° for 20-25 minutes. In a double boiler mix 1 stick margarine, 3 tablespoons cocoa and 5 tablespoons milk, bring to boil; add the sifted powdered sugar, vanilla and pecans. Use as frosting.

CHICKEN ENCHILADA CASSEROLE

1 chicken, boiled, skinned, boned, & cut into bite-sized pieces	1 can Old El Paso enchilada sauce, mild
1 cup shredded cheese	1/2 tsp garlic salt
1 cup mushroom soup	1 can chopped green chilies, optional
1 small onion, chopped	
1 pkg dip size Fritos	
1 cup chicken broth	

Combine all but Fritos and broth, mix well. In a casserole dish layer Fritos, chicken mixture, Fritos and mixture. Pour broth over all. Bake at 350° for 30 minutes. Serve hot.

CHICKEN CASSEROLE

1 medium onion, chopped	1 can (4 oz) chopped green chilies
3 Tbs butter	1 cup sour cream
1 can chicken broth	1 lb cheese, grated
1 can enchilada sauce (or 1 small can of tomato paste and 2 cans of water)	1 chicken, cooked, boned & cut up
	1 pkg corn tortillas (or Tostadas or Fritos)

Brown onion in butter, add broth, sauce and green chilies; cook over low heat for 15 minutes. Mix sour cream and half of the cheese; cook over low heat until cheese melts. Combine two mixtures, add chicken and stir. In shallow cake dish layer tortillas and then sauce, repeat. Top with remainder of grated cheese and bake at 350° for 30 minutes.

KASAFF'S STEW

2	lbs beef, bite-sized pieces	4	cloves garlic
1	Tbs oil	1-2	pints red wine
1	Tbs butter		Small whole onions (to
$^1/_4$	lb bacon, diced (or 3 Tbs bacon		taste)
	drippings)		Carrots, cut up (to taste)
1-2	cans tomatoes		Celery, sliced (to taste)
2	cubes beef bouillon	3-4	bay leaves
$^1/_2$	cup boiling water	6-8	cloves

Mix the beef, bacon, oil, butter and drippings in large kettle and brown. Then add the other ingredients and simmer for 5-6 hours.

BILL WORKED AT DISNEY'S with a Russian named Kasaff, who left Russia during the 1917 Revolution. This is Kasaff's recipe, great food for little money.

BRUNSWICK STEW

$1^1/_2$	lbs ground beef	2	cups finely chopped onion
$^1/_2$	lb ground pork or veal	$^1/_4$-$^1/_2$	cup vinegar
1	can corn		Salt & pepper to taste
1	can tomatoes		Tabasco sauce to taste
2	cups finely chopped celery		

Put meat into boiler, cover and place over low heat. Stir often and cook until meat separates, then add other ingredients as listed. Cook slowly until everything is done. Add enough water to make it a little juicy. Serve over rice, top with Chinese noodles.

This recipe was given to me by Pauline, a lady who for many years worked for Bill's aunt in Atlanta. She spent one whole afternoon typing it for me. I still have that typed copy. We all had great affection for Pauline.

SAUSAGE CHEESE BALLS

1	lb sausage
10	ozs grated cheese
$2^1/_2$	cups Bisquick
$^1/_3$	cup water
1	can chopped green chilies
	(optional)

Bland or familiar foods calm.
Spicy or unusual foods stimulate.

Mix all well, roll into 1-1$^1/_2$ inch balls. Bake on greased cookie sheet at 400° for 10-12 minutes.

CAA TRAIL RIDE

JACK SCHWABACHER'S QUARTER CIRCLE FIVE RANCH, near Daniel, Wyoming, was the site of the 1973 ride. It was so nice, we rode there again in 1982. Before the 1973 ride, the Clymers hosted an open house at their home in Teton Village.

The first morning when we went to breakfast, the cook said, "Someone over there is really sleeping. I've been hearing him for two hours, fifty yards away." A few minutes later George Marks came crawling out of his tent.

Both times we camped on the Green River in rendezvous country. The second camp was in a high meadow next to a mountain stream; beautiful scenery and great fishing. In fact, when Bill Moyers, Jack Swanson and Grant Speed went fishing, Bill laid his rod down to go over and help Grant. When he looked back down stream, he saw a moose swimming across the river right on course to his fishing line. Yep, he hooked a moose, but when the animal reached the opposite bank, Bill's six-pound test line broke and the moose went on. That's really "a big one that got away."

One ride out of camp was hard and hot. Upon returning to camp everyone tried to cool off. John Justin stripped off, sat down in the six-inch-deep creek and proceeded to bathe. If anyone would like some photographic reproductions, contact the writer.

Co-foremen on the ranch were Sonny Clements and Darrell Winfield, one of the "Marlboro" men. Darrell was assigning mounts; he roped a horse and said, "Give this one to Watson, it's gentle as a dead hog."

In 1982, some members' sons and grandsons were among the guests: Cashe Swanson, Steve Snidow, Bill Owen, John and Chas. Moyers and Clint Bowden (Warren's grandson).

It was on that ranch that Robert Lougheed said, "The trail ride's one of the most important things in CAA; that's where members get to know one another, get to caring."

There was a soft misty mountain rain; that's where "Watson, Watson & Watson" was photographed, see Snidow.

PLUM SAUCE

2 cups catsup	¹/₂ Tbs salt
²/₃ cup sugar	2 tsp liquid smoke
2 Tbs Hoisin sauce	2 cloves garlic, minced
2 tsp sesame oil	¹/₃ cup cider vinegar
¹/₂ Tbs minced fresh ginger	

Mix well. That's right, no plums.

ONE OF FRED'S FAVORITE DISHES is ribs, especially at Kimo's in Lahaina, Maui. Those Hawaiian fellows like ribs, too. This sauce recipe is printed in *A Taste of Aloha*.

MAHOGANY CHICKEN WINGS

1¹/₂ cups soy sauce	³/₄ cup cider vinegar
³/₄ cup dry sherry	6 large cloves garlic, minced
1¹/₈ cups Hoisin sauce	¹/₂ cup honey
³/₄ cup chinese Plum Sauce	6-7 lbs chicken wings
14 green onions, minced	

When cooked, wine loses most of its alcohol, leaving flavor and calories.

In 3-quart saucepan, combine all ingredients, except wings. Bring to boil and simmer 5 minutes. Cool. Cut off wing tips, disjoint wings and place in large storage container. Pour cooled sauce over wings, cover and refrigerate overnight. Place oven racks at upper and lower thirds. Oil two large, shallow roasting pans. Drain wings, save sauce. Divide wings between two pans and bake in preheated 375° oven uncovered for 1-1¹/₂ hours. HOWEVER, baste about every 20 minutes with remaining sauce and turn frequently to brown evenly. Be sure to switch pans halfway through cooking. Remove wings, cool on sheet of foil. When cool, wrap and store; may be stored for up to 3 days. May be frozen. Serve at room temperature. Serves about 20.

Plum Sauce: In case you can't find it.

²/₃ cup canned purple plums or stewed fresh, sweetened	¹/₄ tsp soy sauce
1 Tbs brown sugar	1 Tbs cornstarch
1 Tbs wine vinegar	2 Tbs water

Combine first four ingredients and heat. Make a paste of last two ingredients, add to first mixture and cook until thickened. Serve.

CHILIES RELLENOS

1 can whole green chilies	2 Tbs flour
¹/₂ cup jack cheese, grated	¹/₄ tsp pepper
4 eggs, separated	¹/₂ lb jack or cheddar cheese,
¹/₂ tsp salt	cut into 3" x ¹/₄" sticks
2 Tbs water	

Beat egg whites until frothy. Add water and salt and beat until stiff, not dry. Add flour and pepper to yolks and beat until thick and lemon colored, fold into whites. Pour 4 mounds (¹/₂ cup each) onto a hot greased griddle. Brown lightly on the bottom (meanwhile, stuff hollowed-out chilies with cheese sticks), then gently top mounds with stuffed chilies. Divide remaining mixture over chilies, be sure chilies are covered. When underside is brown, gently turn and brown other side. Sprinkle with cheese and serve at once. May be topped with taco sauce or hot green chili relish. Serves 2.

STRAWBERRY CREAM BAVARIAN

1 pkg (3 oz) strawberry gelatin	6 Tbs sugar
1 cup boiling water	1 pint whipping cream, whipped
1 pint strawberry yogurt	1 angel food cake, broken into
4 cups sliced fresh strawberries	1-inch pieces

Dissolve gelatin in boiling water; chill until consistency of unbeaten egg whites, whip until frothy. Combine sugar and fresh strawberries. In order, fold the yogurt, strawberries, whipped cream and cake into the frothy gelatin. Pour into unusual-shaped dish. Refrigerate overnight. Freeze if desired. Unmold, garnish with more whipped cream and fresh strawberries.

EASY LEMON CHICKEN

2 lemons	2 Tbs margarine
2 chicken breasts, skinned, boned & halved	2 Tbs brown sugar
¹/₄ cup flour	1¹/₂ tsp salt
¹/₂ tsp paprika	¹/₂ cup chicken broth

The best way to reply to a non-believer is to give him a good dinner and ask if he believes there is a cook.

Grate rind from one lemon, set aside. Squeeze juice from one lemon over chicken. Mix flour and paprika and coat chicken with mixture. Brown the chicken in margarine in large skillet. Sprinkle chicken with lemon rind, sugar and salt, add broth. Reduce heat, cover and cook for 25 minutes. Slice second lemon, arrange over chicken and cook 10 minutes more. Serve. Serves 4.

BROILED TUNA-CHEESE SANDWICH

1 cup tuna	¹/₄ tsp salt
¹/₂ cup grated cheese	4 slices bread
¹/₄ cup chopped chives or green onions	1 egg white
	¹/₂ cup mayonnaise

Mix tuna, cheese, chives and salt; spread on bread. Beat egg white until stiff. Gently fold in mayonnaise; spoon onto tuna mixture. Broil until tops are puffy and golden brown. Serves 2-4.

CAA TRAIL RIDE

CHARLIE SCHREINER III hosted the 1974 ride at his historic YO Ranch in the Texas hill country near Mountain Home. Some highlights were the longhorn drive, the nighttime wild boar hunting and the exotic game.

Grant Speed borrowed a horse from his uncle. As Grant was leaving the ranch, driving down the road alongside the ostrich pasture, a big rooster ostrich jumped to its feet right next to the fence line and so frightened Grant's horse that it caused the trailer to become unhooked and turn upside down over the horse. The animal fought its way out of the contraption and headed back toward YO head-quarters. Eventually, the trailer was righted, rehitched and the horse reloaded. Next time, Grant stood on the side of the trailer and "flagged" the horse until they were past the ostrich pasture. Even after they got out on the highway, the horse was still so hyper that the slightest thing seemed to spook him. Once, the horse got so worked up they pulled over on the shoulder and when the trailer gate was opened, the horse reared over back-wards out onto the ground. Grant stayed with the horse, there along the road, while his uncle went to the nearest town to get a veteri-narian. The vet came out and gave the horse a tranquilizer injection. That's how the story got started that Grant Speed had to "shoot" his horse on one of the trail rides.

C.D. McGehee, of the YO, took Snidow and me out to see the ostrich nests; when the big "red-necked rooster" showed up, I outran both of those young men back to the pickup. The doctor for that ride brought along a number of drugs and not hav-ing anyplace to carry them, put them into Melvin Warren's saddlebag. Later in the day, Mel checked his saddlebag. He wondered who the wise guy was and what kind of trick he was trying to pull; so, he just threw all those little bottles away. That evening Doc asked Mel if he could get his medicine out of the saddlebag. "So that's what that was," Mel said, and told the doctor what had happened. Don't know if Doc ever found all the vials or not.

Poker was almost always dealer's choice, another rule Polk didn't like. One game, "Up & Down the River," involved an ante and nine bets. Tom Ryan won it so often we began calling it "Long Tom."

Snidow found a vertebra and a broken arrowhead. By using a bit of mud, he was able to make it look as if the arrowhead was embedded in the bone. Some of the artists envied Gordon, until the mud dried and the arrowhead fell off. But the "seed" was growing. In 1981, we returned to the YO for a second ride; all 24 CA members were present that year. Again, we had a longhorn roundup and trail drive, a most picturesque sight, one you never get tired of. There was also some team roping in YO's new arena.

NBC's "Today Show" was there and reported on the ride and the groundbreaking for the Cowboy Artists of America Museum in Kerrville.

One night we went up to the main house to see our host's gun collection. Red Steagall was the last one to find cover as "Three" cranked off a few blank rounds from the Gatling gun; the wadding ricocheted off the vault door and down the hallway.

It rained both times, that's why Schreiner keeps inviting CA back.

CHEESE APPETIZER

8 ounces brie cheese   **1   can Pillsbury crescent rolls**

Spread the dough out to approximate the shape of the cheese: wedge, square or circle. Place the cheese in the middle of the dough and fold edges up around the cheese. Bake at 350° for 15 minutes, or until lightly browned. Serve with crackers or raw vegetables (one of Fritz's favorites). Camembert cheese may be used.

If an egg floats in fresh water,
it's wise not to use it.

SWEET BAR-B-QUE SAUCE

1 **large onion, minced or ground**	**¼ tsp rosemary**
2 **cloves garlic, minced or ground**	**¼ tsp thyme**
½ **cup raisins, minced or ground**	**¼ tsp marjoram**
1 **large bottle (44 oz) catsup**	**3 Tbs brown sugar**
1 **tsp dry mustard**	**Juice of ½ lemon**
⅔ **cup butter**	**¼ tsp black pepper**
½ **tsp basil**	**1 tsp salt**
1/4 **tsp tarragon**	

Combine all ingredients. Boil gently for 45 minutes, stir often. Can be easily doubled or quadrupled. Keeps very well in the refrigerator. We use it on ribs or chicken.

GERMAN STUFFING FOR TURKEY

1 **egg, beaten**	**½ envelope Lipton onion soup mix**
4 **cups bread crumbs**	**½ cup unpopped popcorn**
½ **cup chopped celery**	

Combine all ingredients. Stuff and bind up foul. Bake at 375° for 3 hours. When the 3 hours are up, get the hell out of the kitchen because that popcorn is going to blow that turkey's rear-end right out of the oven.

WHEN FRITZ'S FATHER, Denver White, passed away, we came upon an old, handwritten, family cookbook. This recipe was among them; it's typical of the sense of humor I love in Fritz and Denver.

It might have been easier for Fritz to have done a "pop-up bronze" than a drawing.

FRITZ'S FRESH FRUIT TORTE

CAKE:
- 1   pkg Jiffy yellow cake mix
- 2   Tbs water
- 1   egg
- 2   Tbs butter
- 2   Tbs brown sugar
- 1/2   cup chopped nuts, optional

GLAZE:
- 1/2   cup apricot preserves
- 2   Tbs water

FROSTING:
- 12   ozs cream cheese
- 1/2   cup sugar
- 1   tsp vanilla

FRUIT:
- 1   pt small strawberries, whole
- 2   bananas, sliced
- 1   can pineapple chunks
- 2   kiwi, sliced
- 1   pt blueberries, whole

Mix cake ingredients; pour onto a greased and lightly floured pizza tin and spread it out thin. Bake at 375° for 15 minutes; cool. Cream the frosting ingredients and spread over cooled cake. Lay fruit on frosting in circles, spokes, initials, brands, etc. Be creative. Boil glaze until preserves are melted; drizzle over fruit. Refrigerate an hour or two before serving.

CHOCOLATE ZUCCHINI CAKE

3/4 cup brown sugar
1/2 cup sugar
1/2 cup (1 stick) butter
1/2 cup oil
3 eggs
1 tsp vanilla
1/2 cup buttermilk
2 1/2 cups flour

1/2 tsp allspice
1/2 tsp cinnamon
1/2 tsp salt
2 tsp baking soda
4 Tbs cocoa
2 cups grated zucchini
1/2-1 cup chocolate chips

Cream together the sugars, butter and oil. Mix eggs, vanilla and buttermilk. Combine the two mixtures. Sift and mix all dry ingredients (flour, spices, salt, soda and cocoa). Combine everything, except chips, and mix well. Pour into a greased 9-x-13-inch pan and bake at 325° for 45 minutes. Put chocolate chips on top.

WHITE SAUCE

2 Tbs flour, sifted
1 cup stock, milk or cream

2 Tbs water, cold

Combine flour and water, milk or cream. Mix until smooth, add stock and heat. Simmer until proper consistency.

JELLO ICE CREAM PIE

1 #2 can* pineapple chunks
1 small pkg lime Jello
1 pt vanilla ice cream

1 pie crust (graham cracker, vanilla water or chocolate wafer)

Drain pineapple, save juice and add enough water to make one cup, bring to boil; dissolve jello and stir in ice cream until blended. Chill twenty minutes, fold in pineapple and pour into crumb crust. Chill until firm. May substitute frozen raspberries and raspberry jello, mandarin oranges and orange jello, or whatever you like.

CRANBERRY-ORANGE RELISH

1 lb raw cranberries, ground
1 #2 can* crushed pineapple

2 oranges, ground, rind too
2 cups sugar

Mix all ingredients well and refrigerate at least overnight. Serve with turkey.

*See Appendix.

28

CAA TRAIL RIDE

DICK WOOTTEN AND BILL REARDON of the Y7 Red River Ranch, near Springer, New Mexico, were very capable hosts in 1975.

Lots of activities were available, including team-roping at a neighboring ranch. The cowboys admitted the artists won the roping, Fred Fellows headin' and Bill Owen heelin .

Reardon had brought a case or two of "blue rock" and many boxes of shells. Five people, two ranch hands and three of CAA's group shot three out of three. Next, Fred drug out an antique, five-shot riot gun. Only three people got five out of five, the three from CAA's group.

They had some mountain oysters, which Reardon didn't know how to cook; Fellows said, "Go get Watson." We put about one inch of Wesson oil in an iron skillet and heated it just short of smoking. The casings of the mountain oysters were split and removed. The delicacies were dipped in beaten eggs, dredged in a mixture of this much Bisquick and that much garlic salt and placed into the hot oil. When the edges were brown, the meat was turned, once. When done, they were placed on paper towels and lightly sprinkled with garlic salt.

I'd found a buffalo vertebra, at a piskun (buffalo jump) near Three Forks, Montana, drilled a hole in it, filed the hole into shape and pounded an arrowhead snuggly into the opening. Snidow took the vertebra, along with some pottery pieces, to Wootten in October of 1974; they "salted" a cut bank. The stuff laid there all winter. On the ride, some people went artifact hunting; Harvey Johnson was the lucky finder, but unfortunately not everyone was a good enough actor and eventually Johnson caught on. The "perpetrators" were getting better though, more authentic.

As trail riders were leaving the Y7, one of the cowboys brought out a bullwhip. It was handed to Fellows, he snapped it a couple of times and cut first one, then a second piece of paper from Snidow's hand. When the whip was returned to the cowboy, he just coiled it up and walked back toward the bunkhouse.

Fred Fellows brought along a large tepee called the "Montana Hilton." Guest Ed Thrasher filmed the 1975 ride for CAA. And the weather was beautiful.

Before the ride, the Moyers and Lougheeds both hosted open houses. Fritz White wore his purple cowboy outfit to Lougheed's.

BUD'S BARBEQUE SAUCE

2   Tbs salad oil
1   medium onion, chopped
3   cans tomato sauce
1   cup vinegar

$^1/_2$ cup molasses or firmly packed
     brown sugar
2   Tbs Worcestershire sauce
1   tsp coarse black pepper

Sauté onions in oil for about 10 minutes. Add rest of ingredients and simmer for 45 minutes; if it gets too thick, more water may be added. Excellent on chicken or ribs.

SWEET AND SOUR SPARERIBS

2   lbs spareribs cut into 2" lengths
1   tsp pepper
1   tsp salt
1   large onion, sliced
2   Tbs brown sugar
2   Tbs cornstarch
$^1/_4$ cup vinegar

$^1/_4$ cup cold water
1   cup pineapple juice
1   Tbs soy sauce
2   green peppers, cut into
     large pieces
6   pineapple slices, cut into
     chunks

Put spareribs in kettle and cover with water. Add salt, pepper and onion and cook until almost done. Drain and brown in broiler. Mix sugar, cornstarch and 1 tsp salt in large skillet; stir in vinegar, cold water and soy sauce. Cook slowly until juice becomes transparent. Add green peppers and cook for about 3 minutes. Add pineapple chunks and juice and heat through only. Drain ribs, add them to sauce. Very good served with rice. Serves 3-4.

POTATO CASSEROLE

2 potatoes	1 cup milk
6 ozs sliced, fully cooked Canadian bacon or ham leftovers	³/₄ tsp salt
¹/₂ cup chopped green onion	¹/₂ tsp marjoram
³/₄-1 cup shredded sharp cheddar cheese	Dash pepper
5 eggs	Parsley

Cook potatoes in jackets until tender. Peel and slice into ¹/₂ - inch slices. Make alternate layers of potatoes and meat in baking dish approximately 12-x-8-x-2-inches. Sprinkle onion and cheese over top. Combine remaining ingredients and pour over all. Bake at 375° for 30-40 minutes. Garnish with parsley. Can be assembled ahead of time and refrigerated. Serves 4-6.

STEAK AND MUSHROOM CASSEROLE

6 Tbs flour	3¹/₂ cups water
6 Tbs oil	1 large round steak
1 large onion, sliced	Salt & pepper to taste
¹/₄ lb mushrooms, sliced	Johnny's seasoning salt

Cut meat into 6 equal pieces. Flour, lightly salt and brown quickly in 4 Tbs oil. Remove from skillet to casserole. Add rest of oil and 6 Tbs flour to skillet to make a thin paste. Add water and thicken to a thin gravy. Seasoning salt to taste. Spread onions and mushrooms over meat, pour gravy over all. Cover and bake at 350° for 1¹/₂ hours, or until tender. Serves 6.

PRAIRIE BERRY CASSEROLE

3 Tbs oil	¹/₂ cup catsup
¹/₃ cup chopped onions	3 Tbs vinegar
1 clove garlic, minced	1 Tbs dark brown sugar
1 16-oz can pork & beans	1 Tbs powdered dry mustard
1 16-oz can lima beans, drained	Salt & pepper to taste
1 16-oz can kidney beans, drained	

Heat oil in skillet, add onions and garlic and sauté. Combine catsup, vinegar, sugar and mustard. Put beans in 2-quart casserole, add all ingredients and stir. Cover and bake at 345° for about 45 minutes. Serves a bunch.

Bud Helbig

BLOODY BASIN BURGERS

1 lb ground beef	2 thick slices Jack cheese
4 strips bacon	1 ripe avocado, sliced
1/2 red onion, sliced	Lawry's salt and pepper to taste
1 clove garlic, chopped	

Fry bacon strips; add onion and garlic, sauté and set aside. Make beef into two patties and fry, seasoning each side to taste. When done, cover with cheese, avocado and bacon, pour on onion and garlic; cook just a couple of minutes more. Serves 2.

BILL AND I HAVE DONE a lot of camping. One spring we were out in Bloody Basin; it had drizzled all night and morning. When we stopped for lunch all the wood was wet and there were mighty slim pickin's in the chuckbox. Bill got a very good fire going and I came up with "Bloody Basin Burgers."

FLAUTAS

2 lbs boned chicken breasts or rump roast	18-20 corn tortillas
2 cloves garlic, chopped	1-2 cups lard (tastes better) or shortening
Ground pepper & seasoned salt, to taste	

Simmer meat in seasonings, with enough water to cover, until tender. Let cool and then flake meat. Dip all tortillas, one at a time, in hot lard, not too long though—you want them soft so they won't crack when rolled. Then put about 2 tablespoonfuls of meat on each tortilla, roll and fasten with a toothpick. Fry tortillas 3-4 seconds on each side in hot lard. Serve with guacamole and salsa. Serves 1 man, 1 woman and 1 child. I figure 7-8 tortillas per man, 5-6 per woman and 2-3 per child. This dish is best prepared outside in a cast iron skillet. It tastes better and the grease splatters don't need to be cleaned up.

MARGARITA'S GUACAMOLE

2-3 fresh soft avocados	2-3 canned jalapenos, chopped
4 Tbs sour cream	2 Tbs jalapeno juice from can
1 bunch green onions, chopped	2 Tbs fresh cilantro, or 1 1/2 Tbs dried
4 cloves garlic, finely chopped and mashed	Salt to taste, optional

Blend together all ingredients by hand with a fork, like I did before we got electricity, or in a blender, but be careful, texture is important. You'll find that dropping one of the avocado pits into the mixture will help keep it from browning so fast.

SALSA FRESCA

5-8 fresh tomatoes
1-2 bunches green onions
3-5 fresh guero (wax) chilies
3-5 fresh California chilies
2-4 fresh jalapeno chilies

Lots of fresh cilantro
1 large fresh clove garlic
3-4 Tbs salad oil
2-3 Tbs white vinegar (Regina, if possible)

When a cook cooks a fly, he always keeps the best wing for himself.

Finely chop all ingredients. Mix and eat. Better the second day, if it lasts, even on eggs. In case you haven't noticed, fresh is the key word in this recipe. But, if fresh isn't available, used canned or dried. This takes some time but it's worth it. Vary the mixture, you'll find your favorite.

SON-OF-A-GUN STEW

1 lb kidney tallow, cut into small pieces
5-6 feet marrow gut, cut into 2-inch pieces
$\frac{1}{2}$ kidney, cut into small pieces
1 pair sweetbreads, cut into small pieces
Water

Small amount liver, cut into small pieces (optional)
1 set brains, cut into small pieces
All the butcher's steak, or 1 lb flank steak
3-4 potatoes, optional, cubed
Flour
Salt & pepper to taste

Put tallow into hot Dutch oven; flour all the other meat pieces (except brains), brown well in hot tallow. Add enough water to cover. Keep good heat on and under oven; cook 8-9 hours adding water as needed. Add potatoes last two hours; add brains last hour of cooking. If necessary, add more flour to make gravy; salt and pepper to taste. Must be eaten with Dutch oven biscuits and butter. Serves 8-10.

DUTCH OVEN BISCUITS

3 cups unbleached flour, or $1\frac{1}{2}$ cups wheat flour and $1\frac{1}{2}$ cups white flour
4-5 Tbs sugar

3 Tbs baking powder
$\frac{2}{3}$ cup (about) butter flavored Crisco
1 cup (about) buttermilk

Sift dry ingredients together in a large bowl. Cut Crisco in with fork until crumbly; add enough buttermilk to make dough workable. Dump dough out on floured board, roll and cut biscuits. Place in well-oiled hot Dutch oven (hot lid too). Keep moderately hot, top and bottom, until browned (15-18 minutes).

CAA TRAIL RIDE

MANY C-BERS CONVERGED on Barbara and Wayne Wallace's Diamond W Ranch, south of Sanders, Arizona, for the 1976 "ride."

There was a shortage of horses that year and it is sometimes referred to as the "CAA Trail Walk." We were camped on a scenic hillside with only one tent for shelter and one for the kitchen. However, as usual, we had a great cook and fantastic food. The team ropers got in some action at a neighboring ranch, but the main activity was a roundup and branding. The only relief from the heat was a bath in a nearby tank.

CB Handles: Snidow (Brown Jug), Beeler (Banjo), Fellows (Montana Roper), Warren (Zip Lip), Owen (Wild Turkey; Gobble-Gobble), Niblett (Choctaw Kid), Moyers (Ol' Paint), Polk (Peaseful Polk) and Watson (White Elephant).

BOB SHELTON, OF THE KING RANCH, invited CAA to Valentine, Texas, in 1977. Bubba Whitehead and Mac Sproul actually handled the ride on that part of the Running W. The King Ranch, famous for its cattle and horses, also had a number of excellent riding mules.

We camped in a small canyon, which had once been a Texas Ranger's camp. There were a number of buzzard roosts on the cliffs around camp, but by the end of three days without baths, we'd driven them off. Everyone was advised to bring cots to sleep on as there were lots of snakes; the only snake I saw that whole trip was within the city limits of Midland.

There were lots of canyons with high rocky bluffs where one could look a great distance at the varying landscape. Valentine is just north of where the movie "Giant" was filmed. The country was described as having Snidow fences, Boren buildings and McCarthy rocks.

Frank Polk was always pushing to get a poker game started. That year he took along a card table and one chair. (He could only use one chair so why bring more?) With the card table, chair and cot in the car, there was no room for the spare tire, so Frank left it at home.

Bubba had placed a generator about 100 yards up the road so we could have electric lights scattered around camp. The generator actually caused more of an incentive to go to bed than it did to stay up, because whoever was last to turn in had to walk up the road, switch off the generator and stumble back to camp in the dark.

En route, Bill Owen, Fred Fellows, Bud Helbig and guest Ed Thrasher paid $5.00 to a store clerk for a liquor advertisement of a life-sized woman. During the ride, they kept talking about the woman in camp. Some of the riders never saw her until the group photograph in that year's catalog. Gary Niblett didn't care if there was a woman in camp or not, he'd heard there was to be an initiation.

RED CABBAGE

1	medium head red cabbage, shredded	1	tsp sugar
2	Tbs flour	1/4	cup vinegar
1	tsp salt	1	Tbs bacon drippings or oil
1/8	tsp pepper	1	large apple, grated
1/2	cup water	1	large onion, grated

Place cabbage in ice water for 5 minutes or more. Mix all other ingredients in crockpot, cover and set on high. Drain cabbage well and add to crockpot, mix thoroughly. Cook on high for 20 minutes, reduce to low and cook for 3-4 hours. Best made a day ahead of time and reheated. Serves 8.

POTATO PANCAKES

2	lb potatoes, grated	1 1/2	tsp salt
1	small onion, grated	1/2	tsp black pepper
3	eggs, beaten	1/2	tsp baking powder
3/4	cup flour		Oil for frylng

Grate potatoes into a bowl of ice water, let sit. Mix all other ingredients into a batter. Drain potatoes well, press out all liquid and add them to batter. Spoon heaping tablespoonfuls into frying pan and flatten into 3- to 4-inch round patties with back of spoon. Brown on both sides, drain on paper towels. Can be made ahead of time and frozen. If frozen, defrost in refrigerator, place on cookie sheets and bake at 375° for 10-15 minutes. Makes about 15.

APPLE CAKE

1	cup butter or margarine	1	tsp cinnamon
2	cups sugar or 1-1½ cups honey	⅛	tsp nutmeg
3	eggs	2	tsp vanilla
3	cups sifted flour	2	cups chopped walnuts
1½	tsp baking soda	3	cups chopped, skinned apples
½	tsp salt		

Beat butter and sweetener until well combined; add eggs one at a time, beat well after each, then add vanilla. Combine dry ingredients and add gradually to the first mixture. Fold in apples (McIntosh are good) and nuts. Mix well. Batter should be extremely thick. Pour into greased and floured tube pan. Bake at 325° for 1½ hours. Let cool at least 15 minutes before removing from pan. Serve plain or iced. Serve this as dessert, after saurbraten.

10-DAY SAUERBRATEN

3	cups vinegar	½	cup flour
3	cups water		Shortening for browning
6	bay leaves	½	cup each: chopped onion, celery
20	whole peppercorns		& carrots
6	whole cloves	¼	cup dry red wine
2	tsp thyme		Salt, pepper & sugar, as needed
1	onion, chopped		for gravy
7+	lbs bottom round beef		

Combine first seven ingredients and heat to boiling. Place meat in large non-metal container, pour in marinade, cover and refrigerate for ten days. Be sure there is enough marinade to cover half the meat. Rotate meat once each day. Remove meat and drain. Strain and save marinade. Flour meat and brown in shortening. Remove meat to platter and cook vegetables in pan, covered, for about 10 minutes. Return meat to pan, add strained marinade and wine. Cover and bake at 325° for 2½-3 hours. Remove meat to platter, cover with foil and keep warm. Strain liquid in pan; if it is too vinegary, dilute with water. Add flour, salt and pepper as needed to make gravy. Serves 8.

Most recipes refer to large eggs,
about 2 ounces each:
Jumbo eggs, 30 oz/Dozen
Extra large eggs, 27 oz/Dozen
Large eggs, 24 oz/Dozen
Medium eggs, 18 oz/Dozen

NUT CAKE

6	extra large eggs, separated	4	cups ground hazelnuts or other
¹/₂	cup plus 1 Tbs honey		nuts
1	tsp dried lemon peel		Crisco
1	Tbs lemon juice		

In medium bowl, beat egg whites until stiff. In large bowl, beat egg yolks one minute, then slowly add honey; beat on high till puffy—about 5 minutes. Add lemon peel and juice, beat till blended. Fold in nuts with spatula, then fold in whites. Grease 9¹/₂-inch spring form tube pan, line bottom with wax paper and grease. Pour in batter. Bake on middle rack of oven at 350° for about 40 minutes or until cake pulls away from sides of pan. Serve with whipped cream.

PECAN COOKIES

1	cup butter or margarine	2	cups flour
¹/₂	cup sugar	2	cups chopped pecans
1	Tbs water		Extra sugar
1	tsp vanilla		

Cream butter until soft; add sugar and beat until fluffy. Blend in water and vanilla. Combine flour and nuts and add to creamed mixture. With lightly floured hands, break off small pieces of dough and shape into small rolls. Place 1 inch apart on ungreased cookie sheet. Bake at 350° for 25-30 minutes, or until very light brown. While still warm, roll in granulated sugar. Makes about 7 dozen.

EASY HUNGARIAN GOULASH

2	lbs beef stew meat, 1" squares	¹/₂	tsp pepper
¹/₄	lb bacon, 1" pieces, fried crisp	1	clove garlic, crushed
1	lb sliced onions	1	tsp caraway seed
2	Tbs red sweet paprika	1	can beef consomme
2	tsp salt	1	Tbs flour

Sprinkle a little flour into the skillet before frying bacon, eggs, chicken, etc., and the grease won't pop so much.

Place stew meat on waxed paper, season with salt and pepper. Sauté onions in bacon fat, cook till soft; add paprika, stirring to dissolve. Add meat, cover and simmer about 15 minutes. Add garlic, caraway seed and only enough consomme to barely cover meat; add more consomme as needed. Simmer 2 hours or until meat is tender. Then dissolve flour in consomme or water, stir into goulash to thicken. Cook 5 minutes longer. Serve with rice or noodles.

CAA TRAIL RIDE

ONE OF THE OLDEST DUDE RANCHES in Wyoming is the HF Bar, fifteen miles north-west of Buffalo, at a beautiful little place called Saddlestring. That's where CAA went in 1978 for a no-host ride: wives and children went too. Dean Thomas, who had wrangled dudes for years, made sure everyone had a good time. Every cabin was right on, or over, the creek.

That was Red Steagall's first ride and several times we were entertained by his guitar playing and singing.

In the main dining room, they served fantastic homestyle meals, but those weren't any better than the ones served on the cookouts.

There was team-roping too, but roping was becoming an annual event on CA rides.

It was learned that one of the guests, Lindy Bates, used pine cones to make wreaths. While riding around the mountainsides John Clymer, Harvey Johnson, Bob Lougheed and Dean Thomas came upon a lot of eight- to ten-inch cones. They hand-picked a couple of burlap bagfuls and presented them to her.

It rained and hailed, which can make for a very exciting ride.

ZOFIA'S CHOICE
(Polish Strawberry Crepes)

CREPES:

6	Tbs flour, sifted
2	eggs
2	egg yolks
2	cups milk
1	tsp sugar
1/2	tsp salt
1/4	cup butter, melted

STUFFING:

2	cups sliced strawberries, or 1 frozen pkg
1/2	cup sugar

TOPPING:

1/2	pt sour cream
1/2	cup sugar
	Cinnamon to taste

CREPES: Mix flour, eggs and yolks, add milk, sugar and salt; beat with mixer at low speed for 2 minutes. Heat a 4-inch skillet and brush with butter. Pour 1 tablespoon of batter into the pan and immediately tilt pan so the batter spreads over the entire bottom; cook to a golden brown. Stack on a plate. Repeat until all the crepes are cooked. Yields about 12 crepes.

STUFFING: Mix strawberries and sugar (frozen berries should be thawed). Lay a crepe brown side up, put in stuffing, fold sides over and sauté in butter until golden on both sides.

TOPPING: Combine ingredients, mix well. Serve each crepe with a dollop of cream on top; may be topped off with a whole strawberry.

KRYSHA'S QUICHE

2	large leeks	8	large tomatoes or red peppers,
3	Tbs butter		hollowed out
3	slices bacon		Pinch nutmeg
4	large eggs	$^1/_2$	tsp fresh ground pepper
1	cup half & half	$^1/_2$	cup grated parmesan cheese
1	tsp salt		

Trim roots from leeks and cut lengthwise leaving a little green. Mince leeks and sauté in butter until soft, but not mushy. Cut up bacon and sauté until partly cooked. Drain bacon and combine with leeks. Beat eggs, half and half, salt, pepper and nutmeg and combine with bacon and leeks, mix well. Stir in cheese. Spoon mixture into tomatoes or peppers. Bake at 375° for 25 minutes, or until set and peppers are done. Serves 8.

KRYSHA HAS A DEFINITE TASTE of her own which doesn't include crust of any kind. This is her creation.

NIBBLETTES

3	medium eggs	$^1/_4$	cup soft butter
2	egg yolks	1	lb lard, or shortening
$^1/_4$	tsp salt	$^1/_2$	cup confectioner's sugar
2	cups all purpose flour		Powdered vanilla to taste,
$^1/_4$	cup vodka		if you can get it

Beat eggs, egg yolks and salt until creamy; add sugar and beat some more. Add flour, vodka and butter; knead the dough for 10 minutes. On lightly floured board roll out small portions paper thin, cut into $1^1/_2$-x-6-inch strips. Cut a 2-inch slit in the middle of each strip then pass one end of the strip back through the slit. Heat the lard in a large frying pan. Fry strips on high heat on both sides until golden; place on paper towel to cool. Using a sieve, sprinkle strips with additional confectioner's sugar; mix sugar with powdered vanilla to taste. (Chrust-Faworki is a traditional Polish treat for winter parties.) Yields 3 dozen.

WINE JELLO

2 envelopes unflavored gelatin	1 pint red wine
¹/₂ cup cold water	3 lemons, juiced & strained
2 cups grape or cranberry juice	Fresh fruit
³/₄-1 cup sugar	Powdered sugar

Dissolve gelatin in water. Put fruit juice in a pan and bring to a boil; add dissolved gelatin. Add the sugar and dissolve. Let cool; add the wine and lemon juice. Pour into a chilled mold and refrigerate until set. Unmold. Decorate with powdered-sugar-coated fresh fruit, serve.

POLISH TACOS

1 can (6¹/₂ ozs) tuna in spring water, drained	1 tomato, diced
1 small onion, diced	¹/₂ cup grated cheese
1 small clove garlic, minced	6 Taco shells (I use blue corn)
¹/₂ cup picante sauce	Lettuce, shredded
	Small amount of diced cilantro (optional)

Sauté onions and garlic until transparent, add tuna, picante and cilantro and heat. Serve in taco shells topped with tomato, cheese and lettuce. Spanish rice and a salad always go well with these. Low cal and delicious. Polish accent not guaranteed, neither required nor acquired.

POLISH PICKLE SOUP

¹/₂ lb beef or chicken, cubed
¹/₂ cup sliced celery
¹/₃ cup diced carrots
²/₃ cup chopped onion
1 cup cubed potatoes, raw
¹/₄ tsp pepper
4 cups water
3 Tbs sour cream
1 large dill pickle, grated
Pinch salt

Dead wines are wines fortified with brandy, resulting in sherrys and ports, which have a higher alcoholic content; they don't spoil. Living wines are all others, which should be served at 50° to 60° temp.

Slowly cook meat and raw vegetables in 4 cups water with salt and pepper. Simmer gently until vegetables are tender. Be sure the potatoes are done, then add grated pickle. Stir in sour cream just before serving. Serves 4.

CAA TRAIL RIDE

Between the Gallatin and Madison rivers, an hour's drive north of Yellowstone National Park, lie two well-known ranches, the "Spanish Creek" and the "Flying D." Both are owned by Bob Shelton and he invited CAA to hold its 1980 ride there.

It was on the "Flying D," in 1979, when CAA President Gordon Snidow and I, the Secretary-Treasurer, were checking out possible campsites and activities, that Shelton asked if CAA would be interested in having a museum in Kerrville, Texas. During the 1980 ride, some future founders met with CAA and the concept of a Cowboy Artists of America Museum was agreed upon.

Besides the hillsides covered with cattle, good mounts and lots of wildlife, there was an open-pit agate mine, a stone fetish and Ruby Mountain. Ruby Mountain was actually a hillside where you could pick "Montana Rubies" (garnets) up off the ground. Napi, the stone fetish, about eight feet long, was located high on a bluff— from there you could see the piskun (buffalo jump) near Logan.

Some riders used Fred Fellows's "Montana Hilton" again. Anglers needed only to take about ten steps to the stream behind the bunkhouse to go fishing. On one outing, riders witnessed a rare sight—an eagle's mating flight.

Of course it rained; look at the trail ride photos in the catalog.

BILL ABSOLUTELY LOVES BREAKFAST! He sculpts into the early hours of the morning and doesn't get to sleep until 2 or 3 A.M. He starts his day around 9 or 10 A.M. When he does get up, he wants a huge breakfast. Bacon or sausage, eggs, hashbrowns, and pancakes or waffles. His favorite pancake is what his grandfather called German pancakes; most people refer to them as crepes. He loves to eat but doesn't want to make a ceremony of it.

GERMAN PANCAKES

2	cups Bisquick	1	Tbs cinnamon
1¹/₂	cups milk	1	Tbs sugar
2	eggs		

Combine all ingredients in large bowl. Whisk until mixture is smooth, should be the consistency of sauce instead of a regular pancake. I use a small iron skillet, one of the most important ingredients of this recipe. The pan must be heated to a high heat. Put enough vegetable oil in the pan to cover it lightly, pour enough batter into the pan to thinly cover the bottom, and while you are pouring the batter, tilt and move the pan so the batter spreads the same thickness over the entire pan. When the pancake is golden brown, turn it over gently. Repeat this process. They should be very thin. Serve with butter and corn syrup, sugar or jam.

FOODS THAT ARE FAST AND EASY are what he prefers. Time taken out for a long and elaborate meal is just time away from one of the many projects he always has going. About the only times we have large fancy meals are on holidays.

Bill's a meat and potato man. He'd rather eat hamburger than any other meat, with wild game brought home from one of his hunting trips coming in second.

Hunting is Bill's favorite activity. Most of our family outings revolve around some hunting or shooting event. He has made each of us our own custom rifle, with name and birthdate engraved in the barrel.

Bill's favorite type of food is Mexican, with tacos being first choice. But to get that recipe you'll have to go to your local Taco Bell and ask the manager; by the way, if

Got something TOO salty?
If time is short, put in a bit of brown
sugar. If you have plenty of time,
put in some quartered potatoes,
cook, remove the potatoes
and serve your dish.

you have any luck, please let me know as I've been trying for years. The one homemade Mexican dish Bill really enjoys is my Chili Con Carne. I got the recipe from a Mexican family I lived with during my junior high school days in the Verde Valley. I use venison, elk or antelope meat in this recipe, but beef may be substituted.

CHILI CON CARNE

2 **lbs venison (beef), diced**	6 **cups water**
3/4 **cup flour**	2 **Tbs veg. shortening**
2 **Tbs chili powder**	**Salt and pepper to taste**

Using a large iron skillet, brown the meat in the shortening. Mix the flour and chili powder in large bowl. Add 2 cups water to the mixture and stir until smooth. Pour the mixture over the browned meat and add the remaining water, mix well. Simmer for about one hour or until the sauce has thickened to your preference. Season to taste.

I serve this with flour tortillas, over chili rellenos, or as a side dish with Bill's favorite, tacos. Serves 4.

ANOTHER FAVORITE IS PASTIES. Made from an old family recipe my ancestors used, it stems from the mining towns of England, Ireland and Wales. It's a meat pie without any gravy; the left-overs were taken down into the mines for lunch. My mother and grandmother always made individual pies with our initials on them. I've begun teaching our children how to make them so the tradition can go on.

PASTIES

FILLING:

3 **lbs venison (beef), diced**
2 **onions, diced**
5 **large potatoes, diced**
1 **cube butter**
    Salt and pepper to taste

CRUST:

5 **cups flour**
1 **Tbs salt**
3 **cups vegetable shortening**
    Water

Place the meat, onions, and potatoes in separate bowls; cover potatoes with water so they don't turn brown.

Crust: Mix flour and salt in a large bowl, work the shortening into the flour, one cup at a time, until the mixture is similar to small grains of rice. Then add just enough cold water to make the mixture stick together. Work the dough as little as possible, as working makes it tough.

Strong herbs: use one level teaspoonful per four servings. Medium herbs: use one heaping teaspoonful per four servings. Delicate herbs: use all you want.

For individual pasties take some dough, about the size of a baseball, and roll it out on a floured board to the size of a large pie pan. Then, on half of the rolled-out dough, first spread a layer of meat, next onions and potatoes last. Then put a few pats of butter on top of the potatoes, salt and pepper and fold over the other half of the dough, making the pastie take on the shape of a half circle. Pinch the edges together. Slit the top of the pastie once or twice to let moisture out. Repeat the process until all the ingredients are used. Makes four or five pasties. Place them on a large baking sheet and bake at 350° for 1 hour and 15 minutes, or until done. Serve with a salad.

CAA TRAIL RIDE

ONE OF THE COUNTRY'S GREAT CATTLE RANCHES, the Kokernot o6 Ranch at Alpine, Texas, hosted the 1983 trail ride. Chris Lacy, a Kokernot descendant, headed up the ride with able assistance from cowboss Joel Nelson. The cowboys do their work in the traditional way on the spread of 220 sections.

The riders went along with a chuck wagon and a remuda of 40-odd horses and two mules, riding over rugged rangeland to a high plateau where camp was set up.

Excellent, traditional trail ride meals were prepared by well-known range cook Ramon Hartnett.

Ken Riley and Frank McCarthy got their fill of riding iron-wheeled chuck wagons over rocky ground and of opening barbed wire gates. Harvey Johnson chose to return by powered vehicle when he decided that the horse offered him would provide more rodeo than ride. That was the first CAA trail ride for Mehl Lawson, Gary Carter and Robert Duncan.

A couple of the guests tied their mounts to a windmill and climbed upon the tank. The passing chuck wagon spooked the tied horses they broke the reins and ran on ahead to the fenceline where a lot of others were waiting. In the excitement Hampton got "unhorsed"; that didn't happen in Montana, but John was ten years younger then.

The '83 trail ride capped off a week of activities marked by the official opening of the Cowboy Artists of America Museum in Kerrville, Texas; Museum Director Griff Carnes was a CAA guest on the o6. En route, over half the people got tickets at a "roadside rest stop/speed trap." However, a friendly Texan came to our rescue.

MARLIES' HORS D'OEUVRES

1	8-oz pkg Philadelphia cream cheese, whipped	1	tsp Worcestershire sauce
8	ozs (1 cup) sour cream	6	ozs cooked ham, diced
1	Tbs curry powder	1	cup Baker's coconut, sweetened
		1	apple, diced

In a large bowl, combine cheese, sour cream, curry and Worcestershire, mix. Add ham, coconut and apple; mix thoroughly. Serve with pumpernickel or rye bread. May be made a day in advance, BUT don't add the apple until just before serving. Serves 8.

BEDROLL CHICKEN

3	whole chicken breasts	12	oz sour cream
1	lb bacon, thin slices	1	pkg ham, thin slices
1	lb fresh mushrooms, sliced Toothpicks		Worcestershire sauce

Skin and bone chicken; cut into twelve pieces. Wrap each piece with 2 or 3 strips of bacon; put a dash or two of Worcestershire on each. Place the slices of ham on the bottom of a 2- to 3-inch-deep baking dish. Put chicken pieces on top of ham. Pour liberal amount of sour cream over all. Cover with aluminum foil and bake at 325° for 1 hour. Remove foil, add mushrooms on top and bake one hour more uncovered. Serves 4-6.

OLD-FASHIONED GERMAN SAUERKRAUT

3	lbs sauerkraut, drained
$\frac{1}{2}$	lb sliced bacon, cut into $\frac{1}{4}$" strips
1	cup old-fashioned Grandma's molasses, or dark brown sugar
3	apples, peeled & quartered
$\frac{1}{4}$	cup wine
1	tsp caraway seeds

Brillat-Savarin (1755-1826), French lawyer and gourmet, wrote, "Fowls are to the kitchen what canvas is to the painter."

Fry bacon crisp. Save fat, drain bacon on paper towels and set aside. Put all other ingredients into a pressure cooker and cook for 15 minutes, cool immediately. Add one-half the bacon to the other ingredients and brown in a large skillet, in the fat. Sprinkle the remaining bacon on top and serve.

Or, instead of pressure cooking, put one-half the bacon and all other ingredients into a large casserole dish and bake at 325° for $2\frac{1}{2}$-3 hours; baste with wine. Sprinkle the remaining bacon on top and serve. This will keep for up to two weeks refrigerated. Serves 8.

BRAISED STUFFED FLANK STEAK

1	lb ground round	1/2	cup beef broth
2	eggs, slightly beaten	2 1/2	lbs flank steak, all fat removed
3/4	cup chopped onion	1	Tbs oil
1/2	rib celery, chopped	2	Tbs butter
1	Tbs parsley, chopped	3/4	cup finely chopped carrots
1 1/2	tsp salt	2	bay leaves
1/2	tsp fresh ground black pepper	3/4	cup chopped onion
2	cups 1/2" bread cubes, no crust	1	large tomato, skinned & chopped
3	Tbs butter	1	tsp thyme
1/4	cup oil	1/2	cup dry red wine

Have the butcher cut a large pocket in the steak. Combine the stuffing ingredients through black pepper and toss to mix. Heat 3 tablespoons butter and 1/4 cup oil, add bread cubes and sauté until golden brown; drain cubes. Combine the bread and stuffing; fill steak pocket. Lap the steak over pocket opening and tie every few inches to form a bundle or loaf shape; season with salt and pepper.

In a large deep casserole heat the remaining butter and oil and brown the meat bundle on all sides. Then add remaining ingredients, except broth and wine, and cook over medium heat 5 minutes. Add broth and wine, bring to boil, cover and simmer for 1 1/4 hours. When done, transfer the meat to a warm platter, remove the string and keep meat warm. Strain liquid and serve with salad and scalloped potatoes. Serves 6-8.

LEMON BLUEBERRY CAKE

2	eggs
1/2	cup water
	Oil
1	box Duncan Hines lemon cake mix
1	can blueberry pie filling

In a bowl, combine the mix, eggs and water; pour into an oiled rectangular cake pan. Pour the pie filling over the cake mix and swirl with a knife. Bake at 350° for 40 minutes or until done.

To keep fruit and nuts from sinking to the bottom of cakes, muffins, breads:

1

Heat them in an oven before adding them to the mixture; or,

2

Lightly flour them before adding them to the mixture; or,

3

Add them to the mixture last, just before baking.

TRAIL RIDE COOKIES

2¹/₄ cups whole wheat flour	1 tsp salt
¹/₂ tsp baking soda	¹/₂ cup butter, softened
1¹/₂ cup brown sugar	3 eggs
1 tsp vanilla	12 ozs chocolate chips, semi-sweet
1 cup chopped peanuts	1 cup sunflower seeds, shelled

Combine flour, salt and soda in a bowl. Mix butter and sugar in a large mixing bowl; add eggs and vanilla, mix. Stir into the dry mixture. Finally, add the chips, nuts and seeds. Place by spoonfuls on baking sheet. Bake at 375° for 10-15 minutes. Makes about 60 cookies.

PEACH OMELET

3 medium eggs, beaten	2 Tbs margarine
1 cup Bisquick	¹/₈ cup vegetable oil
2 16-oz cans sliced peaches, drained	Sugar for topping

Add Bisquick to beaten eggs. Melt margarine in large skillet over medium heat, add oil. Pour Bisquick mixture into hot skillet, spoon peaches onto mixture, cover skillet and cook about 7 minutes. Remove from stove, slide omelet onto a large plate. Turn skillet upside down over plate, grasp opposite sides of both the plate and skillet with hot pads, and turn over quickly so omelet is inverted in skillet. Cover and cook the second side about 7 minutes. Return to plate and sprinkle with sugar. Serves 4.

CHICKEN IN BARBECUE SAUCE

8 chicken breasts, boned & skinned, cut into 1" strips	2 green peppers, chopped
	1 large onion, chopped
1 28-oz bottle of Hunt's barbecue sauce, all natural, original recipe	8 mushrooms, sliced
	¹/₄ cup margarine

Melt 2 tablespoons margarine in large pot, add strips of chicken and stir until brown, reduce heat. Drain off liquid, pour in barbeque sauce and simmer for 30 minutes. In a large skillet, sauté the peppers, onion and mushrooms in 2 tablespoons margarine for about 15 minutes. Pour vegetables over chicken, mix and cook for 5 minutes. Serve over rice or noodles. Strips of sirloin may be used instead of chicken. Serves 6.

THUNDERBIRD SALAD

SALAD:

$^1/_2$ head lettuce, cut fine
1   large tomato, diced fine
1   avocado, diced fine
$^1/_3$ cup chopped green onion
8   strips bacon, crisp & crumbled
$^3/_4$ cup fine chopped celery
$^2/_3$ cup crumbled blue cheese

DRESSING:

$^1/_3$ cup salad oil
$^2/_3$ cup rice vinegar
$^1/_3$ tsp pepper
1   Tbs lemon juice
1   clove garlic, crushed
$^1/_2$ tsp salt

Mix the first six ingredients together in bowl. Sprinkle the cheese on top.

SALAD DRESSING: Combine ingredients, mix well; pour over top of salad and toss. This recipe was created by Gary's mom and dad while working at the Thunderbird Country Club in Palm Desert, California. Serves 4.

EXOTIC CELERY

4   heaping cups celery, cut in $^1/_4$"-$^1/_2$" pieces
1   can cream of chicken soup
1   large jar pimentos, with liquid, chopped
    Water

1   can sliced water chestnuts, drained
    Pinch salt
1   cup slivered almonds, sautéed in butter

Boil celery in water for 8 minutes, drain well, add everything else except nuts, mix and place in 2-quart casserole. Sprinkle nuts on top and bake uncovered at 350° for 30 minutes. Try it before you judge it. Serves 4-6.

BEST-EVER PIE

1   cup raisins
4   eggs, separated
1   Tbs butter
$1^1/_2$ cups sugar
$^1/_2$ tsp cinnamon

$^1/_2$ tsp ground cloves
3   tsp vinegar
1   cup chopped walnuts
1   unbaked pie shell

Add water to raisins, bring to boil and cook for 1 minute; drain and cool. Beat egg whites until stiff, set aside. Beat egg yolks, butter and sugar together. Add spices and vinegar. Fold in beaten whites, walnuts and raisins. Pour mixture into pie shell and bake at 350° for about 1 hour.

CARROT PUDDING

2 cups finely grated raw carrots	¹/₂ cup finely chopped suet (shortening can be used)
1¹/₂ cups brown sugar	
1 cup buttermilk	3 eggs, beaten
1 tsp baking soda	1¹/₂ cups flour
1 cup chopped walnuts	2 tsp baking powder, mixed into flour
1 cup bread crumbs, dry & fine	
1 tsp cinnamon	1 cup currants
¹/₂ tsp nutmeg	¹/₄ tsp allspice, optional

Stir soda into buttermilk. Combine remaining ingredients. Blend in buttermilk and soda. Spoon into favored mold or a coffee can. Steam for 2 to 2¹/₂ hours. Check after 2 hours. Pudding should be moist, not dry. Serve with sauce. Serves 8 to 10.

SAUCE

1 cup sugar	4 egg yolks
1/2 cup butter	1 cup cream

Cream sugar and butter together; when light and fluffy, add egg yolks, one at a time, mixing after each. Mix in cream. Cook in double boiler or over very low heat, stirring constantly until thickened. Warm when ready to serve; DO NOT BOIL or it will separate. Serve on Carrot Pudding.

BROWN SUGAR SAUCE

2 cups water	1 tsp nutmeg
1 cup brown sugar	1 tsp vanilla
1 stick butter	3 Tbs cornstarch

Mix cornstarch and a little water, set aside. Combine all other ingredients in a saucepan, bring to boil, add cornstarch mixture. Cook to desired thickness. Serve on Carrot Pudding.

SPANISH QUICHE

2 cans (8 oz) whole green chilies, opened and seeded
8 ozs Monterey Jack cheese, grated
7 slices bacon, fried crisp, crumbled
6 eggs, beaten
Dash nutmeg, or two

Beating separated eggs, beat the whites first and then the yolks; DON'T clean the beater in between the two.

Line 9-inch pie pan with split chilies, in lieu of crust. Sprinkle cheese over chilies. Add nutmeg and bacon to beaten eggs. Gently spoon the mixture over the cheese. Bake at 350° for 45 minutes or until inserted knife comes out clean. Serves 6-8.

SWEET POTATO SALAD

1 can (1 lb 10 oz) sweet potatoes, mashed	1/4 cup mayonnaise
1/2 cup finely chopped celery	1/4 cup Durkee's famous sauce
3 green onions, cut up	Salt & pepper to taste
2 sweet pickles, diced	1 hard-boiled egg, sliced
2 hard boiled eggs, chopped	

Combine first eight ingredients, mix well. Chill. Garnish with egg slices: Serves 6.

WHEN GARY WAS ABOUT 19 and going to college in California, he claims he was so poor he worked two jobs to survive. In the mornings he pumped gas and in the evenings he worked at a pizza parlor for meals. His boss often lamented not paying him a salary. When Gary arrived at work he would make a large pizza, limited only by the size of the oven and pizza paddle, and eat it. During work he was forever sampling ravioli and spaghetti and had lasagna for dessert. When he finished work he'd make another large pizza, loaded, cut it up to fit into a box and then take several pitchers of flat beer and pizza to his "deli-smelling" room. At six A.M. Gary would get up, have cold pizza and flat beer for breakfast and go forth to pump gas. The combination of gasoline, pepperoni and anchovy was so overwhelming, hardly anyone lingered long enough to talk, let alone argue. Even the insects stayed away, as his whole body exuded an Italian seasoning's aroma.

About six months later he landed a more lucrative job at another gas station. After closing up the station at night, Gary would go around to a certain drive-in just as it was closing and the girls would give him all the cold hamburgers and french fries that had been cooked ahead but hadn't sold. He lived on those until the school year ended.

Gary claims the only thing that straightened out his eating habits was a hitch in the U.S. Army. (Is that possible?) Today Gary doesn't complain about food and has never sent anything back to the Chef. As far as he's concerned, everything is delicious.

JOHN WAYNE CASSEROLE

12	ozs chopped green chilies, drained	4	eggs, separated
1	lb Monterey Jack cheese, coarsely grated	1	Tbs flour
1	lb cheddar cheese, coarsely grated	$^1/_8$	tsp pepper
$^2/_3$	cup evaporated milk	2	tomatoes, thinly sliced
		$^1/_2$	tsp salt, optional

Blend chilies and cheeses and put into well-buttered shallow casserole. In small bowl combine milk, egg yolks, flour and pepper, blend. In large bowl beat egg whites to stiff peaks. Using rubber spatula, gently fold whites into yolk mixture. Then pour over the cheese and chili mixture and carefully blend. Bake at 350° for 30 minutes, remove from oven and add tomatoes over the whole top, return to oven and bake 30 minutes more, or until inserted knife comes out clean. Serves 6-8. A friend told me this was one of Wayne's favorite dishes, hence the name.

John Wayne was an Honorary Member of CAA from May 20, 1967, until his death.

CURRIED PUMPKIN SOUP

$^1/_4$ cup ($^1/_2$ stick) butter
1 large onion, diced
$^3/_4$ cup sliced scallions, white
    pods only
1 16-oz can pumpkin
4 cups chicken stock
1 bay leaf
$^1/_2$ tsp sugar

$^1/_2$ tsp curry powder
$^1/_4$ tsp nutmeg
Few sprigs parsley, chopped
2 cups whipping cream or half &
    half
Salt & pepper to taste
Sour cream, paprika & chopped
    chives for garnish

Over medium high heat, melt butter in a 4-quart saucepan and sauté onion and scallions until soft. Stir in other ingredients from pumpkin to parsley. Bring to simmer, reduce heat and simmer, uncovered, for 15 minutes, stirring occasionally. Remove bay leaf. Puree mixture in blender. Return to saucepan, add cream, salt and pepper and simmer 5-10 minutes, DO NOT ALLOW TO BOIL! Serve with a dollop of sour cream sprinkled with paprika and chives. Serves 4.

Fresh eggs are rough and chalky in appearance; older eggs are smooth and shiny.

DAN'S MIX

1 cup mayonnaise
1 Tbs mustard
$^1/_2$ tsp pepper (no salt)

1 Tbs finely grated onion
1 Tbs finely chopped parsley greens
1 Tbs finely chopped celery greens

Combine and mix well. Delicious over beef, pork or chicken.

AMAZING PIE

$^1/_2$ cup Bisquick
4 eggs
$^3/_4$ cup sugar
$^1/_4$ cup margarine (not butter)

2 cups milk
1 tsp vanilla
Dash nutmeg

Put all ingredients into a blender; set on mix and run for 5 minutes. Pour into greased pie pan, preferably pyrex. Bake at 350° for 45-50 minutes. Use your imagination for topping: whipped cream, pie mixes, shaved chocolate, etc. It is especially good in a shortcake. There is a very similar recipe called IMPOSSIBLE PIE: substitute $^1/_2$ cup flour and $^1/_2$ Tbs baking powder for the Bisquick, increase the vanilla to a tablespoonful and add 1 cup coconut. When baked, there will be a crust on the bottom, custard in the middle and toasted coconut on top.

BARBARAQUE SAUCE

$^1/_4$ cup honey	1 Tbs soy sauce
8 ozs tomato sauce	1 clove garlic, minced
$^1/_4$ cup lemon juice	$^1/_2$ tsp Tabasco
1 Tbs Worcestershire sauce	

Mix well. Store in refrigerator.

BEAN DIP

1 can bean dip	1 8-oz pkg cream cheese
$^1/_2$ pt sour cream	Shredded Jack and cheddar
$^1/_2$ pkg taco mix	cheeses

Blend first four ingredients. Bake in casserole dish at 350° for 30 minutes. Sprinkle cheese on top and stir to blend.

NEVER-FAIL CHICKEN AND DUMPLINGS

1 medium chicken	4 tsp baking powder
Salt & pepper to taste	1 egg
2 cups flour, sifted	1 cup milk
$^1/_2$ tsp salt	

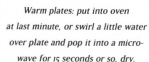

Warm plates: put into oven at last minute, or swirl a little water over plate and pop it into a microwave for 15 seconds or so, dry.

Season chicken with salt and pepper and boil until tender. Bone chicken and cut into small pieces. Return chicken to broth and set aside. Sift together flour, salt and baking powder. Break egg into measuring cup, beat lightly and fill cup rest of way with milk; add to the dry mixture and beat a little. Cover dough and let set five minutes. Drop dough by the tablespoonful into boiling chicken and broth. Cover and boil for twenty minutes. Even better the next day. Serves 4.

BLACK-AND-BLUE SALAD

12 ozs blackberry Jello	8 oz pkg cream cheese
3¼ cups boiling water	½ cup sour cream
1 can (15 oz) blueberries & juice	⅓ cup sugar
1 can (8 oz) crushed pineapple & juice	1½ cups chopped nuts

Dissolve Jello in boiling water; add blueberries, pineapple and juices. Chill. Mix cheese, cream and sugar; spread over top of Jello. Sprinkle nuts on top.

RACHEL'S REFRIGERATED ROLLS

$1/4$	cup warm water	2	tsp salt
2	cubes compressed yeast	1	cup shortening
$1^1/_3$	cups sugar	2	cups milk, scalded
6	eggs	9	cups flour

Blend all ingredients together; knead in all the flour. Divide into six balls; roll each one into a pie-sized circle and cut into twelve pie-shaped pieces. Roll up each piece, beginning at the wide end. Place on cookie sheet and freeze, store in plastic bag in freezer. Allow to thaw and rise for three hours before baking in a 350° oven for 20-25 minutes. Makes 72. Rachel, my mother-in-law, is an excellent cook. To scald 1 cup milk, cook in microwave for 2-$2^1/_2$ minutes, stir once every minute.

AWFUL-LOTTA ENCHILADA

1	pkg (12) tortillas	1	large onion, diced
1	can (20 oz) Wolf's chili, no beans	3	cups grated longhorn cheese
1	can water		Oil

Combine chili and water, bring to boil and simmer for 10-12 minutes. Put a little oil in a skillet and slowly heat, one at a time, all tortillas, on both sides. Lay a tortilla in a large casserole dish. Put 3-4 tablespoons chili, some cheese and 1-2 teaspoons onion on tortilla. Roll up the tortilla and scoot it to the end of the dish, repeat until all the tortillas are done. Pour the remaining chili down the center of the tortillas and top with the remaining cheese. Bake at 350° for 30 minutes.

CAA TRAIL RIDE

THE FIGURE 4 CENTENNIAL CELEBRATION was in 1984. Waldo and Beldora Haythorn, along with Craig, Jody and Sally, invited CAA to the sandhill cow country south of Arthur, Nebraska, to help get things rolling. Jack Swanson was the only member who couldn't make that ride.

The first morning out, Waldo told the riders they were free to rope anything with four legs and horns. When we arrived at camp, out of sight and sound of roads, high lines and buildings, there was a pen full of steers waiting to be roped; Waldo and Craig, both ropers, understood the desire.

The second morning there was an old-fashioned roundup and branding; the riders gathered about 400 head. Waldo drove a spring buggy pulled by a matched team of black mules, Ruby and Pearl; Gordon Snidow rode beside Waldo and I rode in the back seat. At times there were as many as twelve ropers dragging (once, ten were CAA associated) and nine teams holding. It was the first time Mehl Lawson had "roped and drug" to a branding fire. Waldo allowed all those greenhorns out there because they were backed up by skilled and experienced neighbors and family members. We were through before noon and relaxed until the seemingly truckloads of food were brought in by the ranchers wives and helpers.

A couple of ranch hands went out the first day to dig a trash pit. Later, standing around and telling stories, Howard Terpning, Bud Helbig, Ed Lane, Jim Boren and Griff Carnes were kicking through the sand and began to find bullets, casings, whole shells and uniform buttons; they were the real stuff, authentic. Everyone had seen the cowboys turn over the new sod. The following days they found more, including gun parts, crossed-rifle cap insignias and a brass lyre music holder. The news of the "find" was even relayed to the wives in town. The *Western Horseman* write-up of the ride mentioned the "archaeological dig." Waldo had told some of us there were no historical sites on the 65,000 acres where they raised Belgian, Percheron and Quarter horses and Hereford, Angus, Brangus and Longhorn cattle.

Volunteer Perry Johns came all the way from Fort Worth, Texas, to do the cooking at an authentic chuck wagon setup with tarp cover and cook's tent. When we moved to headquarters, the chuck wagon was pulled by a four-horse hitch of Belgian "blondies," the stove wagon was hooked to that and the remuda and hooligan wagon brought up the rear. When Craig wasn't supervising or helping, he was doing it himself; he was everyplace. At headquarters there were more steers and an arena.

The hosts' dinner for riders, families and guests was prepared by Mr. and Mrs. Clifton Harris who had come over from Harris' Barbeque in Cheyenne, Wyoming.

Okay! Back to the "archaeological dig." It seems Joe Beeler happened into an "antique" shop just after the owner had bought a bag of "goodies." Beeler told the man of his plan, and was able to buy the "treasured pieces" for what the owner had in them ($7.00), providing Beeler would come back and tell how it worked. Using slight of hand and the cover of darkness, Beeler, Fellows, Nebeker and Owen were able to "salt" that trash pit, unseen and unsuspected. When Terpning heard the full story, he sent the "found pieces" to Beeler. Joe returned them to Howard.

The Haythorns had rolled out the carpet and CAA used it, even though it rained.

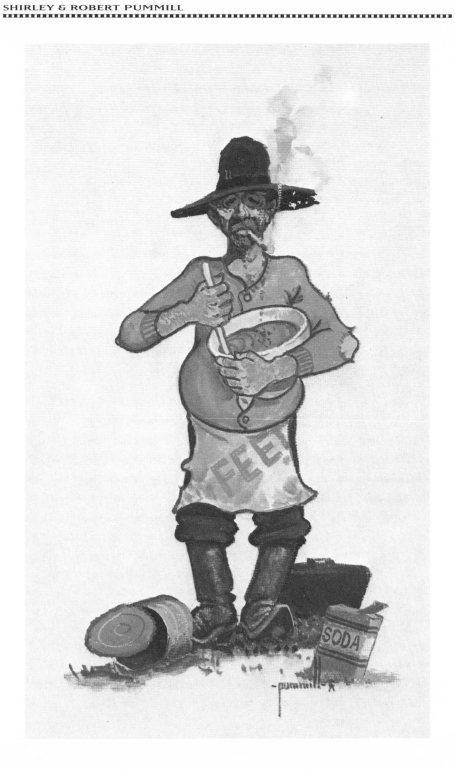

SHIRLEY'S STRAWBERRY SQUARES

1	cup all-purpose flour	1/4	cup brown sugar
1/2	cup chopped walnuts	1	stick margarine, melted

Mix above ingredients and spread evenly into a 13-x-9 x-2-inch pan. Bake at 350° for 20 minutes, stirring occasionally, 3 or 4 times. Cool.

2	egg whites, beaten	2	Tbs lemon juice
10	ozs partially thawed strawberries, or 2 cups fresh strawberries	4 1/2	oz frozen whipped topping, thawed
3/4	cup sugar		

Beat egg whites until stiff but not dry. Add strawberries, sugar and lemon juice. Beat at low speed until thickened (about 2 minutes) then beat on high speed about 10 minutes. Stir in thawed whipped topping. Stir in gently. Crumble baked mixture and spread two-thirds into bottom of a baking pan. Spoon berry mixture on top of crumbs. Sprinkle remaining crumbs on top. Freeze for 6 hours.

CORN CASSEROLE

2	cans cream-style corn	1/2	tsp salt
2	eggs, beaten	1/2	tsp baking powder
1/4	cup yellow cornmeal	8	ozs green chilies, chopped
1/2	cup cooking oil	1/2	lb sharp cheddar cheese, grated
1/2	tsp garlic salt		

Mix all ingredients except cheese. Make 4 alternating layers of mixture and cheese ending with cheese on top. Bake at 350° for 45 minutes.

LIME GELATIN SALAD

1	6-oz pkg lime gelatin	1/2	cup whipping cream
20	large marshmallows	1/2	cup chopped nuts
6	ozs cream cheese		
	Medium can crushed pineapple, drained, reserve juice		

Melt lime gelatin and marshmallows in 3 1/2 cups boiling water. Stir until dissolved and refrigerate until it begins to set. At least one hour before serving, pummel mixture with electric mixer. Soften cream cheese and add enough of the pineapple juice to make it soft enough to whip. Add to gelatin mixture, whipping until well blended. Whip cream and fold into mixture along with the pineapple and nuts. Chill until set.

OLD REPUBLIC INN TORTILLA SOUP

3 qts enriched chicken broth	1 small can green chilies, chopped
2 cups cut celery	4 cloves garlic, crushed
1 can Rotel tomatoes and green chilies, chopped	2 tsp chili powder
	1 tsp sweet basil
2 tsp comino	$^1/_2$ tsp black pepper
1 tsp oregano	$1^1/_2$ pkgs of corn tortillas, cut into strips
2 bay leaves	
16 ozs canned tomatoes with juice, chopped	Monterey Jack or cheddar cheese, grated
4 Tbs honey	Oil
2 cups chopped onion	

Spice up gravies, soups, sauces or boiled white rice by adding one teaspoon wine vinegar while cooking.

Fry tortilla strips in hot oil until crisp, drain on paper towels. Combine all other ingredients, except honey and cheese; bring to boil and simmer about 45 minutes. Remove bay leaves. Just before serving, stir in the honey. Fill bowl with soup; top with tortilla strips and grated cheese. Yields one gallon or more. A favorite in Kerrville.

SPANISH CHICKEN

3 lbs (or so) chicken boiled, boned	1 can (4 oz) green chilies, mashed
18 corn tortilla, in small pieces	1 large onion, chopped
1 small can water chestnuts, chopped	1 stick butter
	1 small jar pimiento, chopped
3 cans cream of chicken soup undiluted	1 medium can mushroom pieces & stems
	1 lb grated cheese

Sauté onion in butter; add all other ingredients, except chicken and cheese, mix well. Slice and/or dice chicken. Layer chicken in two long casserole dishes and add the above mixture. Top with cheese. Bake at 350° for 30 minutes. Serves 12-16.

CAA TRAIL RIDE

TOM CHRISTIAN, owner of the Figure 3 near Claude, Texas, hosted the 1986 ride with the help of Bea and Boone Pickens who furnished some horses from their 2B Ranch. It all started with a brunch and tour at the Panhandle Plains Museum in Canyon as guests of Director Bryon Price. Then on to the Figure 3, part of Charles Goodnight's original JA Ranch, in the Palo Duro Canyon.

Some stayed up on the east rim where the wind blew a bit and where all the meals were served; others stayed down in the canyon at a hunting cabin where other refreshments were served. It took about twenty-five minutes, with four-wheel drive, to make the six-mile ride into or out of the canyon, a ride to be missed. Snidow set a record for driving the route eight times in two days.

They even had a tree-stump target set up for tomahawk-throwing practice.

It was David Halbach's first ride and he spent a lot of time worrying about initiation—he worried about it so much he forgot to look behind him. Initiation consisted of having his gear involuntarily moved from the rim camp to the hunting camp.

A Nashville Cable Network crew was there part of the time, which resulted in two spots on TNN for CAA. Some of the crew members learned not to play "Boo-Ray. "

HERB MIGNERY CA

THE SIX-SHOOTER

1	can (16 oz) pinto beans	1	lb bacon, cut up
1	can (16 oz) pork & beans	1	onion, chopped
1	can (16 oz) red kidney beans		Minced garlic to taste
1	can (16 oz) lima beans	1/2	tsp prepared mustard
1	can (16 oz) white (northern) beans	1/2	cup vinegar
1	can (16 oz) butter beans	1	cup brown sugar

Fry bacon until limp, but NOT crisp. Dump beans, bacon, onion and garlic into a large casserole dish and mix. Combine mustard, vinegar and sugar and simmer 20 minutes. Pour hot liquid over beans and bake at 350° for 1 hour, or until liquid is cooked down to your liking. Stir once or twice. Serves 12.

POTATO SALAD

12	medium-large new potatoes, seasoned, boiled, cubed	1	onion, chopped
6	eggs, hard boiled, chopped		Parsley, chopped, for color
			Salad dressing (see below)

Combine potatoes and eggs and refrigerate until very cold. Add onion and parsley. Stir in salad dressing to your liking. Better if made a day ahead. Serves 12.

SALAD DRESSING

2	cups Miracle Whip salad dressing, do not substitute	1/3	cup whole milk
		2	tsp prepared mustard
1/3	cup Carnation evaporated milk	1/4	cup sugar

Combine all ingredients and mix well. You probably won't use all of this in the potato salad recipe, so store in refrigerator and use in an egg salad or on an egg sandwich.

PICKLED EGGS

1	cup tarragon vinegar	1/2	tsp celery seed
1	cup water	1	clove garlic, minced
2	Tbs sugar	2	bay leaves
1/2	tsp salt	12	hard-cooked eggs, shelled

Combine all ingredients in saucepan, except eggs. Simmer 30 minutes. Remove bay leaf. Cool. Pour over eggs in a crock or jar. Cover and refrigerate 2-3 days before eating.

POTATO SOUP

$^1/_2$	bunch fresh parsley, chopped	$^1/_4$	lb butter
1	bunch green onions, chopped	1	qt half & half
1	cup chopped celery	1	pt milk
4	cups cubed potatoes		Salt and pepper to taste

Sauté parsley, onion, celery, and potatoes in butter until tender. Add milk, half and half, and salt and pepper. Heat, do not boil. Serves 6.

HONEY-GLAZED CARROTS

6	large carrots, julienne	3	Tbs honey
$^2/_3$	cup water	$1^1/_2$	tsp lemon juice
3	Tbs butter		Chives and/or parsley, chopped
	Salt & pepper to taste		

Place carrots in water and cook until water evaporates. Toss carrots with butter, honey, lemon juice, etc. Serves 4-5

NESTER'S CASSEROLE

1	cup onion slices	2	cans tomatoes
$1^1/_2$	cup carrots julienne	$1^1/_2$	tsp salt
1	cup sliced green pepper	1	Tbs sugar
$^1/_2$	cup pimiento	3	Tbs cornstarch
2	cans long green beans, drained	$^1/_4$	cup butter, melted

Mix all ingredients in a casserole dish, cover and bake at 350° for $1^1/_2$ hours.

APPLE PIZZA PIE

PASTRY:

$1^1/_4$	cups unsifted flour
1	Tbs salt
$^1/_2$	cup shortening
1	cup shredded cheddar cheese
$^1/_2$	cup ice water

SEASONING:

$^1/_2$	cup powdered non-dairy cream
$^1/_2$	cup brown sugar
$^1/_2$	cup sugar
$^1/_3$	cup sifted flour
$^1/_4$	tsp salt

TOPPING:

6	cups pared, sliced apples
2	Tbs lemon juice
$^1/_4$	cup butter

PASTRY: Mix flour and salt; cut in shortening until crumbly. Add cheese and mix. Sprinkle water over mixture and shape into ball. On floured surface, roll pastry into a 15-inch circle; place on baking sheet and turn up edges.

SEASONING: Combine all ingredients and mix well. Sprinkle one-half of mixture over pastry.

TOPPING: Cut butter into remaining mixture until crumbly, set aside. Arrange fruit slices, overlapping them, in a circle on pastry. Sprinkle with lemon juice and crumb mixture. Bake at 450° for 30 minutes. Serve warm.

GO ON A HEAD

1 head cauliflower, whole	1 tsp Worcestershire sauce
1 pkg mixed vegetables	1 Tbs minced onion
Water to cover	1 tsp garlic salt
1 cup Miracle Whip	1 Tbs mustard
2 boiled eggs, chopped	

Place cauliflower in pan, cover with water, cook and drain. Prepare mixed vegetables according to instructions, drain. Combine Miracle Whip, Worcestershire, onion and salt; heat. Add mustard and eggs to the hot mixture, mix well. Place cauliflower head in center of serving dish, arrange vegetables around it, pour sauce over all and serve. Serves 6-8.

They didn't send in one recipe using "Herb's Herbs."

If I were to answer the question of food,
I guess I'd admit that it's all been good.

From those "mom's cafes" to hamburger stands,
I've not had a meal I couldn't call grand.

From candlelight meals at quaint little places,
To a home-cooked meal with friend's laughing faces.
Those fried steaks and gravy from the ol' ranch cook
Still make my memory take a second look.

Now, none of the 'bove can compare, I confide,
When ya "noon" on the trail of a long hot ride,

To a sandwich of cheese on wheat bread or bun,
Warmed in a slicker by the hot summer sun.

SCHUELKE FLUFF

1	lb ground round steak	1	large can peas
1	can tomato soup, plus ½ can water	1	can sliced mushrooms and juice
6	slices bacon, cut into small pieces	4	tsp Worcestershire sauce
1	large can peas	1	pkg Rice-a-Roni

Brown ground round; add soup, water, peas, mushrooms, Worcestershire and warm over low heat. Prepare Rice-a-Roni (either chicken, beef or mushroom-chicken flavor) according to instructions; add to meat mixture. Pour combination into shallow ungreased baking dish, sprinkle bacon on top. Bake at 350° for 30-45 minutes, or until bacon is brown. Serves 4.

BEST-EVER POTATO SALAD

10	lbs (50) Idaho potatoes, boiled, cubed	TO TASTE:
1	qt Kraft mayonnaise	Salt
4-6	ozs French's mustard	Pepper
1	small jar diced pimientoes	Dill seed
1	tsp horseradish	Celery seed
3	ribs celery, chopped	Paprika
4-5	chives, chopped	Dill pickle juice
1	dozen eggs, boiled	

Mash 8 eggs; mix with potatoes, salt and pepper. Stir in all ingredients, except whole eggs and paprika, mix well. Cut remaining eggs in half, place on top of salad and sprinkle paprika over all. Cool well before serving. Serves a crowd.

ROLL ON
(German Beef Rolls)

1	large round steak		Soy sauce, to flavor
1/2	lb bacon, cut into small pieces		Cooking oil
	Flour to thicken		Toothpicks
1	onion, chopped fine		

Remove and discard all fat from meat. *Haul-back* and pound steak, on both sides, until thin. Cut steak into 3-4 pieces of nearly equal size. Combine bacon and onion; divide into 3-4 nearly equal portions. Put bacon and onion portions on middle of steak pieces. Roll up steak pieces and secure with toothpicks; brown, slowly, in oil in skillet. Add a little water and soy sauce to taste; cook very slowly for $1\frac{1}{2}$ hours. Remove rolls; add flour to make gravy. This makes the most delicious gravy, goes great with mashed potatoes. Serves 3-4.

JEAN'S TACOS

1	can Hormel chili & beans, heated	1	small can pitted ripe olives, chopped
6	ozs sharp cheddar cheese, grated		
1	tomato, chopped	$\frac{1}{4}$-$\frac{1}{3}$	head lettuce, chopped fine
1	pkg pre-formed taco shells		

Heat 5 shells in oven at 350° for 5 minutes. Fill shells with remaining ingredients, beginning with chili and beans.

TAMALE PIE

1	large can tomatoes (1 lb 13 oz)	1	small onion, chopped
1	cup Wesson oil	1	lb ground round steak
2	Tbs chili powder	1	large can pitted ripe olives
1	cup milk	1	large can creamed corn
2	eggs, beaten	2	scant cups yellow cornmeal
	Salt to taste		

Brown meat and onion, in a pot or large skillet; add everything except cornmeal, milk and eggs, simmer for 15 minutes. Mix milk and cornmeal; pour into meat mixture and mix. Fold in the beaten eggs. Pour all into a shallow baking dish. Bake at 350° for 30-40 minutes, don't overcook. Serves 8.

GERMAN POTATO SALAD

6 medium White Rose potatoes	$^1/_2$ tsp sugar
1 small onion, finely chopped	8 slices smoked bacon
$^1/_3$ cup apple cider vinegar	Salt and pepper to taste

Boil potatoes, but don't overcook; peel and slice them. Cut bacon into small pieces and fry well; when browned add vinegar and sugar (or to taste). Don't get it too sweet. Layer potatoes and onion in bowl, salt and pepper each layer. Pour warm bacon mixture over all. Mix carefully and serve warm. Serves 4.

STUFFED FRENCH ROLLS

18 small French rolls	2 4-oz cans chopped ripe olives
$^1/_2$ lb Tillamook cheese, grated	1 can tomato sauce
$^1/_2$ lb American cheese, grated	2 Tbs vinegar
4 hard boiled eggs, chopped	$^1/_4$-$^1/_2$ cup Wesson Oil
2 green onions, chopped fine	Salt and pepper to taste

Remove the tip of one end of each roll, scoop out center as much as possible. Mix remaining ingredients and stuff the rolls. Place on cookie sheet and bake at 375° for 15-20 minutes. These taste so-de-lis-si-o-so!

OUR FRIEND WANDA'S IMPOSSIBLE QUICHE

12 slices bacon, fried crisp, crumbled	$^1/_3$ cup chopped onion
1 cup shredded cheese, swiss or cheddar	2 cups milk
	$^1/_2$ cup Bisquick
	4 eggs
	Salt & pepper to taste
	Grease

Berry Butter: Blend together 1 stick of unsalted butter or margarine, 1 tablespoon of honey and $^1/_2$ cup of strained berries (be sure to remove the seeds).

Lightly grease a 9- or 10-inch pie plate. Sprinkle bacon, cheese and onion evenly over bottom of plate. Place remaining ingredients in blender and mix at high speed for 1 minute; carefully pour this into the pie plate. Preheat oven to 350°, bake for 50-55 minutes, or until inserted knife comes out clean. Let stand for 5 minutes, cut and serve.

CAA TRAIL RIDE

IN 1987, CAA HAD ITS FIRST HORSELESS PAINTING-and-sketching rendezvous. Everyone gathered at Mary Margaret and Bill Owen's ranch near Dewey, Arizona, for a barbeque and some team roping. Many of the artists also visited the George Phippen Memorial Museum at Prescott. Then they all headed north to John and Sam Kinard's Pine Flat Cattle Company ranch headquarters, forty acres of deeded land surrounded by Kaibab and Prescott national forests, near Williams, Arizona.

At times as many as half a dozen easels were set up to paint the rustic old log buildings, or the cowboys who agreed to pose—possibly for another fifteen minutes of fame. Other artists took their easels to the brink of the canyon, cut out by the Verde River near Perkins, to paint its multicolored walls or some of the other spectacular sights in the Sycamore Wilderness Area.

Arizona artists Ray Swanson and Pat Haptonstall had been voted into CAA and this was their first outing with their fellow artists. Fellows brought along a 16-pound Sharps buffalo rifle, and almost everyone tried his hand at hitting a target some 400 yards away.

John and Sam provided the cook, who served great food under a red-and-white-striped mess tent. They were even thoughtful enough to furnish mobile showers on the back of an eighteen-wheeler.

COWBOY CARAMEL CORN

MELT TOGETHER IN SAUCEPAN:

2   cups brown sugar
1   tsp salt
2   sticks butter
$^1/_2$ cup white syrup
$^1/_4$ tsp cream of tartar

Boil 5 minutes. Remove from heat and add:

1   tsp vanilla
$^1/_2$ tsp baking soda

Stir and pour over:

5-6   qts popped corn
2   cups shelled pecans

Mix well and spread out on two cookie sheets, with sides. Bake one hour in a 200° oven. Stir every 20 minutes while in the oven. Great to nibble on while painting, or to give as a gift.

One-half teaspoon dried herbs will season one pound of meat, one pint of soup or one pint of sauce.

ARIZONA HAM BALLS

2	lbs ground ham	1	lb lean ground beef
2	eggs	$^1/_2$	cup milk
1	cup bread or cracker crumbs	1	Tbs ground onion
1	Tbs catsup	$^1/_2$	Tbs allspice
	Dash salt and pepper		

Blend above ingredients together. Roll into balls the size of walnuts and place on two jelly roll pans. (Could be frozen at this point for later use.) Cover ham balls with sauce made of:

1	cup brown sugar	$^1/_2$	cup vinegar
$^1/_2$	cup water	1	8-oz can crushed pineapple
$^1/_4$	cup catsup	2	tsp dry mustard
1	tsp Liquid Smoke		

Bake at 325° for 1 hour and 15 minutes. Good for a buffet dinner. Serves 10 to 12.

BEV'S BROTHER was named Master Pork Producer in South Dakota, so she included this recipe to honor him.

CHERRY-BERRIES ON A CLOUD

Start this dessert two days ahead of serving.

MERINGUE:

$^1/_2$ tsp cream of tartar	6 egg whites
$^1/_4$ tsp salt	$1^1/_2$ cups white sugar

Beat together cream of tartar,egg whites and salt; slowly add the sugar, one tablespoon at a time, continually beating. Beat until firm. Spread meringue mixture in a buttered 9-x-13-inch pan. Bake at 275° for one hour. Turn off the oven and leave the meringue in the closed oven for twelve hours or longer.

FILLING:

$^3/_4$ cup white sugar	2 cups cream (whipped)
6 ozs cream cheese	2 cups miniature marshmallows
1 tsp vanilla	

Blend sugar, cream cheese and vanilla. Stir into cream and marshmallows. Spread the filling over the meringue layer and chill 12 to 24 hours. Cut into squares. Top each square with a dollop of a mixture made with:

2 cups sliced strawberries, or	1 tsp lemon juice
1 6-oz carton thawed, frozen strawberries	1 21-oz can cherry pie filling

This dessert is so delicious it is worth all the work. You might even have two or three batches, at different stages, going at the same time to serve several days in a row.

RAY'S HOMEMADE ICE CREAM

5 fresh whole eggs	$1^3/_4$ cups sugar
2 qts half & half	1 cup whipping cream

FOR VANILLA ICE CREAM:	FOR CHOCOLATE ICE CREAM:
add 1 Tbs vanilla	Add 1 box ($4^3/_4$ oz) instant chocolate pudding mix

In a large bowl, thoroughly blend ingredients together. Pour mixture into container for ice cream freezer, either hand-cranked or electric, following instructions on the freezer. Eat soon. Serves 12 to 15.

Ray has served ice cream to as many as 95 people at one party.

CAREFREE CHUTNEY CHICKEN SALAD

2 cups diced cooked chicken	1 cup sliced celery
1/2 cup sliced green onions	1/4 cup salted peanuts
1 13-oz can pineapple tidbits, well drained	

Mix together in a large bowl and top with dressing:

DRESSING:

2/3 cup mayonnaise	2 Tbs chopped chutney
1/2 tsp grated lemon rind	2 Tbs fresh lemon juice
1/2 tsp curry powder	1/4 tsp salt

Blend together. Stir into chicken mixture. Chill several hours. Serve on greens. Serves 4. It has an unusual flavor. A refreshing and filling salad.

APPLESAUCE NUT BREAD

1   egg, beaten
1   cup applesauce (3 tart apples
        peeled, cooked and mashed)
3   Tbs butter, melted

In recipes, use baking powder in combination with sweet milk and use baking soda in combination with sour milk, buttermilk or molasses.

Mix together.

In separate bowl mix:

3/4 cup sugar	2 cups sifted flour
1/4 tsp nutmeg	1 tsp cinnamon
1/2 tsp soda	3 tsp baking powder
1 tsp salt	

Combine the two mixtures. Stir in:

1 cup chopped walnuts	1 tsp grated lemon rind

Pour into a greased loaf pan, sprinkle some cinnamon on top and let stand 20 minutes before baking. Bake at 350° for 50 minutes. This recipe is from an *Apple Cookbook Beverly* produced in 1968.

FROZEN MOCHA CHEESECAKE

1¼ cups chocolate cookie crumbs	⅔ cup chocolate syrup
¼ cup sugar	2 Tbs instant coffee
¼ cup butter, melted	1 Tbs hot water
1 8-oz pkg cream chease	1 cup whipping cream, whipped
1 can Eagle Brand condensed milk	

In a small bowl, combine crumbs, sugar and butter. Pat mixture into a 9-inch spring form pan or a 9-x-13-inch pan, covering both bottom and side. Chill. In a large bowl, beat cheese until fluffy. Add milk and syrup. Beat until smooth. In small bowl, dissolve coffee in water. Add to other mixture. Mix well and fold in whipped cream. Pour into chilled pan. Cover and freeze 6 hours. Garnish with additional cookie crumbs.

CORN CREOLE

1 onion, chopped	1½ cups tomatoes, chopped (or sauce)
1 small green pepper, chopped	1 cup cream-style corn
2 Tbs shortening	1 cup milk
1½ lbs ground beef	½ cup cornmeal
1 clove garlic, minced	⅓ cup chopped olives
1 tsp salt	4 Tbs chopped parsley
1 tsp chili powder	

Onion odor can be removed by rubbing fresh loveage, or celery, on your hands.

Fry onion and green pepper in shortening until limp, but not brown. Add beef, garlic, salt and chili powder. Cook slowly for 10 minutes. Add all other ingredients. Pour into baking dish and bake, uncovered, at 325° for 1 hour.

KARO-KORN KRAZY KRUNCH

2 qts popped corn	1⅓ cups pecans
⅔ cup almonds	1⅓ cups sugar
1 cup butter or margarine	½ cup Karo
1 tsp vanilla	

Mix popped corn and nuts. Spread on cookie sheet. In a large sauce pan, mix butter, sugar and Karo. Bring to a boil stirring constantly. Boil for 10 to 15 minutes, stirring occasionally, until mixture turns a light caramel color. Remove from heat. Stir in vanilla. Pour over pop corn and nuts. Mix to coat well. Spread. Cool. Break into pieces. Eat. Leftovers store well in an air-tight jar.

CRANBERRY CREAM MOLD

1 tsp unflavored gelatin	1 cup powdered sugar
1 6-oz can frozen cranberry juice, thawed	1½ cups half & half
	1 8-oz pkg cream cheese

Sprinkle gelatin over juice in a small bowl. Let stand 5 minutes to soften. In a large bowl, beat cream cheese and powdered sugar. Place small bowl in a pan of hot water and stir until gelatin is dissolved. Cool. Beat into cheese mixture. Add half-and-half. Continue beating until smooth. Pour into oiled mold and freeze until firm. Dip mold in and out of hot water to loosen contents.

Drizzle with sauce made of:

1 6-ounce can of thawed frozen cranberry juice
½ cup sugar

Boil to reduce by one-third. Sauce will thicken as it cools.

STUFFED ZUCCHINI BOATS

4 zucchini	1 egg, slightly beaten
¼ lb sausage	½ cup cracker crumbs
¼ cup chopped onion	¼ tsp thyme
¼ tsp salt	Dash garlic salt
Pepper, to taste	½ cup grated Parmesan cheese
½ tsp Accent (optional)	

Bake whole zucchini for 10 minutes. Cool. Cut in half lengthwise and remove the insides leaving the shells intact. Mash the scooped-out portion. Brown sausage and onion, drain. Combine remaining ingredients, except Parmesan cheese, with mashed zucchini. Mix well and fill zucchini shells. Sprinkle with cheese and bake at 375° for 25 to 30 minutes. Serve hot.

WALKING TACO DIP

1 small can refried beans	2 avocados, seeded and mashed
1 cup sour cream, mixed with 1 package taco seasoning	4 green onions, chopped
1 medium tomato, chopped	Grated cheese, to taste

Layer all ingredients in order listed, except cheese. Sprinkle cheese on top. Refrigerate. Serve with chips and salsa.

CAA TRAIL RIDE

AFTER THE 1987 EXHIBITION, a bunch of CAA members and their families went to Hawaii for a trail ride. Early the first morning everyone went to the Parker Ranch Museum for a tour and a film on the history of the area and the ranch, then on to the ranch where they were rounding up and working cattle. Some of the members joined in the activities. Beeler and his horse were attacked by a rogue bull, but after a few light hits and some near misses, paniolos subdued the animal. After the calves were trailed to the shipping pens, we all joined the ranch personnel for a steak dinner cooked right there by the scales and cattle chutes. The tour of the Hue Hue Ranch took us through many of the thirteen climate zones on the island. There we learned more about early ranching in Hawaii, climbed into lava tubes to see the drip tanks that caught rain water run-off and ended up on Kona Beach for a luau. One day the Hale Kea Farms was host to all for a Hawaiian-style rodeo. Some of the members participated in "double-mugging" and "po-y-o," both of which involve steer roping and tying. Other members helped with moving the stock and operating the chutes. That day ended with puu-puus (appetizers) and beef roasted on a spit.

On the Kahua and Ponoholo ranches, with some help from the Kea Hou Ranch, we all saddled up and rode inland, through lush grasses, timber and rain forest. Gary Carter's horse got mired in a bog and in its efforts to get out dumped Gary and almost stepped on him. Gary's hat was stomped on and pushed out of sight into the mud. Later someone saw the edge of the hat brim sticking out of the mire. They retrieved both the hat and the silver-buckled hatband, which are now in the CAA Museum in Kerrville, Texas. A few of the members went on to Kauai for more painting and a tour of the Kipu Kai Ranch. There we saw the best yet use of "strip-grazing." We experienced a West that few mainlanders have even heard about.

MOCHA CAKE

2	Tbs butter	$^1/_2$	cup sugar
1	Tbs flour	4	egg yolks, beaten
$^3/_4$	cup brewed coffee		Vanilla and salt, to taste
2-3	squares bittersweet chocolate, melted	1	pkg thin chocolate cookies (Famous Nabisco), crushed

Make a paste with butter, flour and coffee. Add chocolate. Bring mixture to a boil, cook until thick. Slowly blend sugar into beaten egg yolks. Combine the two mixtures and again bring to a boil. Add vanilla and salt. Alternate layers of mixture and crushed cookie crumbs in a buttered 8-x-8-inch pan. Chill well. May be topped with unsweetened whipped cream.

Vanilla extract is made by soaking the beans of a certain orchid in grain alcohol. A good substitute flavoring can be made by soaking a vanilla bean in a pint of 80 or 100 proof vodka for a couple of months.

GREEN CHILI CHICKEN CHEESE SOUP

1	medium sized chicken	2	cups cream of mushroom soup
1	large clove garlic, minced	$^1/_2$	cup sour cream
2	cups chopped onions	2	cups jack cheese, grated
3	cups mild green chilies, chopped		

In a pot, cover chicken with water and cook until tender. Remove from water. Bone and cut into into small pieces. Cool broth and remove fat. Add garlic and onions to broth and simmer for 45 minutes. Return chicken to broth and simmer for one hour. Add chilies and cook for one more hour. Add mushroom soup and sour cream. Blend and cook an additional ten minutes. Add cheese and allow it to melt. Serve immediately.

CURRIED MAYONNAISE DIP

$^1/_2$	pt mayonnaise	3	Tbs catsup
3	tsp curry powder	1	Tbs Worcestershire sauce
1	medium onion, finely chopped	1	clove garlic, minced

Blend ingredients. Serve as dip for fresh vegetables. Keeps well but must be refrigerated.

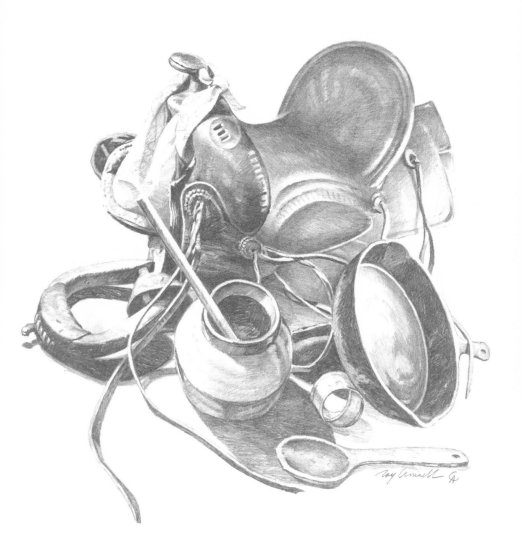

BEST BAKED BEEF BRISKET

4   lb beef brisket, trimmed

MAKE MARINADE BY COMBINING:

1¹/₂   Tbs celery seed

2   Tbs Worcestershire

Pinch of cracked black pepper

¹/₂   bottle Liquid Smoke

¹/₂   tsp meat tenderizer, optional

Pour marinade over brisket. Refrigerate overnight. Turn occasionally. Wrap brisket in foil, to retain marinade. Bake in 225° to 275° oven to desired doneness, 6-8 hours. Cool and refrigerate in order to slice thin. Slice. To serve, heat in 350° oven.

Wild meat usually has much less fat content than domestic meat, so be careful and don't overcook or it becomes too dry.

CHICKEN SPAGHETTI

1   chicken, about 3 lbs

8   ozs spaghetti

1   Tbs butter

1   small can mushrooms, drained

1   small onion, diced

1   green pepper, diced

1   #3 can* tomatoes

Black olives to taste

¹/₂   lb cheddar cheese, grated

Cook chicken slowly in about 2 quarts lightly salted water. When tender, remove chicken from stock. Bone and dice. Cook spaghetti in stock. Drain. Sauté pepper, mushrooms and onion in the butter. Combine this mixture with diced chicken, tomatoes, olives and spaghetti. Pour into greased casserole and bake for 30 minutes in a 350° oven. Stir in grated cheese just before serving.

PICKLED GREEN CHILI

¹/₂   cup sugar

1   tsp salt

¹/₂   tsp mustard seed

¹/₂   cup vinegar

1   tsp dill seed

1   clove garlic, minced

4   cans chopped green chilies

Mix all ingredients except chilies. Bring to a boil. Simmer 5 minutes. Pour mixture over chilies. Cool. Great dip for chips or crackers. Keeps well refrigerated.

*See Appendix.

84

CAA TRAIL RIDE

THE LAST WEEK IN JUNE of 1988, nine CAA members lead a seminar at the Bar N Ranch at West Yellowstone, Montana. Following that they met the other CAA members, friends and families—53 people in all—at Dan and Debbie Leadbetter's Valley Garden Ranch north of Ennis, Montana. The first day we took a tour of Yellowstone National Park in four old 1937 white, open-topped, touring buses.

On the ranch there was a mountain-man camp set up and the 1st Cavalry "K" Troop encampment. One day we had a cattle drive to the Madison River; en route we saw a lot of wildlife, including coyote, deer and eagles. There was roping at the ranch, tours to historic Virginia City and Nevada City and to a piskin (a buffalo jump). On the Fourth of July, "K" Troop led the Ennis parade. CAA members and families, along with the mountain men, entered the parade and won second place in group participation. That afternoon, we went to the rodeo where a few CAA members and friends participated in the team roping events. As trail ride chairman, Gary Carter had gone to a lot of effort to be sure that every place we went we were treated as long-lost friends.

FRIKADELLER
(Danish Meat Balls)

¹/₂	lb ground beef	¹/₄	tsp pepper
¹/₂	lb ground pork	¹/₂	tsp mace
¹/₂	lb ground veal	1	tsp salt
1	onion, minced	¹/₂	tsp coriander
3	Tbs flour	1	tsp thyme
1¹/₂	cups club soda	4	Tbs butter
1	egg, well beaten	2	Tbs olive oil

NOTE: You can use ³/₄ lbs each of beef and pork, but it's better with the veal.

Mix ground meats together (have the butcher grind them together for you). In a bowl, mix meats until well blended. Add onion and flour. Mix well with a wooden spoon. Beat in club soda a few tablespoons at a time. Beat in egg, salt, pepper and spices. Cover bowl with plastic wrap and store in refrigerator for at least one hour (this makes the mixture easier to handle). Shape mixture into 4-x-2-x-1-inch patties. Heat butter and oil in heavy skillet. Add patties 4 or 5 at a time. Cook 6 to 8 minutes on each side until dark brown (never serve rare pork). For a Dane, these should be served with boiled potatoes, cucumber salad and red cabbage.

When a recipe calls for oil, try olive oil, use sparingly. Extra virgin is the best and the most expensive olive oil; then virgin and pure. A rule of thumb: Buy olive oil in glass containers, not tin containers.

CUCUMBER SALAD

1	cucumber	¹/₂	cup vinegar
2	tsp salt	³/₄	cup sugar
¹/₂	red onion	¹/₂	tsp pepper
¹/₂	cup water		

Wash cucumber. Taste skin; if bitter, peel. Score sides with fork or knife. Thinly slice. Mix salt with cucumber slices. Let stand. Slice onion very thin. Separate rings. Squeeze cucumber slices by hand or between two saucers to remove moisture. Rinse in cold water and pat dry with paper towel. Mix water, vinegar, sugar and pepper. Add sliced cucumbers and onion rings. Mix well. Chill before serving. Great with chicken.

STUFFED LOIN OF PORK

NOTE: If you bone your own pork loin, tie every inch or so. Save bone.

4-5 lbs rolled boneless pork loin

MARINADE:

1 cup white wine	2 tsp dry sage
1 large clove garlic, mashed	1 tsp dried thyme
1 bay leaf	Salt and pepper to taste

Mix marinade in large glass bowl. Add pork loin. Cover. Refrigerate overnight. Turn loin from time to time.

FRUIT STUFFING:

6-8 dried apricots	1 Granny Smith apple, cored and
10 pitted prunes	sliced
2 carrots, cut in 2" pieces	$^1/_2$ cup water
1 large onion, sectioned	Dijon mustard
4 Tbs butter, divided	$^1/_2$ cup brown sugar
2 Tbs olive oil	$1^1/_2$ Tbs cornstarch
$1^1/_2$ cups beef broth	3 Tbs water

In a buttered, stainless steel or ceramic roasting pan, brown onions, carrots and bone in a 450° oven for 45 minutes, turning occasionally. If you have vegetables only, use less time. Remove loin from marinade. Pat dry. Make a hole in the center of the loin with the handle of a wooden spoon and stuff hole with prunes, apricots and apple slices. Put 2 tablespoons each of butter and olive oil into a heavy skillet. Add pork loin and brown on all sides. Transfer to a plate. Using the rest of the marinade, deglaze roasting pan. Simmer until liquid is reduced to one-half cup.

Place pork loin, fat side up, in pan. Add broth and water. Bring liquid to a boil. When liquid is hot, cover tightly with foil and braise in a preheated 350° oven for 1 hour or until meat thermometer registers 160°. Transfer loin to an oven-proof dish. Remove strings and brush with mustard. Coat with brown sugar, patting it in firmly. Roast loin in upper third of 450° oven for 15 minutes. Sugar coating should be crisp and bubbly.

Transfer to serving platter, cover with foil and let set for 15 minutes. Strain cooking liquid into sauce pan, adding any melted sugar from roasting pan. Dissolve cornstarch in water. Whisk into gravy. Heat mixture and reduce to a nice consistency. Remove from heat, mix in the remaining 2 tablespoons butter. Salt and pepper to taste. Transfer to heated serving bowl.

This is a fancy version of a Danish Christmas Eve roast. But it is great anytime of the year. Can be made without the marinade, but it really keeps the loin moist and adds so much to the flavor.

RED CABBAGE

1	head red cabbage	
2	cooking apples, peeled, cored, sliced	
2	Tbs butter	
1/4	cup vinegar	

1/4	cup water
1	tsp salt
3/4	cup sugar
1	cup Welch's grape juice

Rinse cabbage. Cut into sections and remove white core. Slice finely in food processor. Melt butter in large sauce pan. Add apples, cabbage, vinegar, water, salt and sugar. Cook 1 1/2 hours over low heat until very tender. Add grape juice the last twenty minutes.

CRYSTAL SHRIMP

1	lb shrimp, shelled & deveined	
4	tsp salt	
1	egg white	
1	Tbs peanut oil	
1	Tbs cornstarch	

3	Tbs peanut oil for frying
1	clove garlic, minced
1	Tbs grated fresh ginger
1	cup snow peas, rinsed
1/2	red pepper, finely chopped

SAUCE:

1	Tbs oyster sauce
1	tsp sesame oil
1	Tbs dry sherry

1/2	cup chicken stock
2	tsp cornstarch

Combine oyster sauce, sesame oil and sherry. Blend small amount of chicken stock with cornstarch. Stir into oyster sauce mix. Set aside.

Put shrimp into large bowl, sprinkle with 1 tsp salt. Mix briskly for one minute. Rinse under cold running water for one minute. Repeat this process two more times. Dry shrimp. Put shrimp into small bowl and sprinkle with remaining salt. Beat egg white lightly and pour over shrimp. Add the 1 Tbs peanut oil to cornstarch. Mix well and combine with shrimp. Refrigerate for one hour.

Beating whole eggs,
add a pinch of cream of tartar.
Beating egg whites,
use a copper mixing bowl
or add a pinch of salt.

Heat wok or skillet. Add remaining 3 Tbs peanut oil. When hot, stir fry shrimp for one minute or until they start turning white. Remove from pan. Adding more oil if needed, heat garlic and ginger until they release their aroma. Add snow peas and pepper. Stir fry for 1 minute. Being sure cornstarch is smoothly mixed, add sauce. Let boil until thickened. Add shrimp. Serve immediately with rice.

SWEET-AND-SALTY POPCORN

2 **sticks butter**	1¹/₃ **cups sugar**
¹/₂ **cup Karo**	**Pan-popped popcorn**

In small saucepan, mix butter, sugar and Karo. Boil well for one minute. Pour over popcorn slowly while stirring and salting to taste.

CANDY BAR COOKIES

32	light caramel candies	1	tsp soda
5	Tbs light cream or evaporated	2	cups flour
	milk	1¹/₂	cups melted butter
1¹/₂	cups brown sugar	1	cup chocolate chips
¹/₂	tsp salt	¹/₂	cup chopped nuts
2	cups quick-cooking oats		

Using a double boiler, melt caramels in the cream. Cool slightly. For cookie layer, combine brown sugar, salt, oats, soda and flour. Add melted butter. Stir until well mixed. Put half of this mixture in bottom of cookie sheet. Bake in 350° oven for 5 minutes. Remove from oven. Scatter chips and nuts on top. Drizzle the caramel mixture over chips and nuts. Pour the other half of the cookie mixture on top and bake for another 15 minutes, until golden brown. Cut into bars.

HONEY CORN BREAD

1¹/₂	cups yellow cornmeal	1	egg, slightly beaten
¹/₂	cup sifted flour	1	cup milk
1	Tbs baking powder	¹/₄	cup butter, melted
1	tsp salt	3	Tbs honey

In large mixing bowl, mix cornmeal, flour, baking powder and salt. In smaller mixing bowl, blend together egg, milk, butter and honey. Combine the two mixtures. Stir just long enough to moisten the dry ingredients. Pour into buttered cake pan. Bake in 425° oven for 20 minutes or until done and golden brown on top. Serve warm with butter, jam, honey, etc., or cold with milk.

CARAMELS

(Read the entire recipe before beginning)

4	cups sugar	¹/₂	lb butter
2	cups white corn syrup	2	12-oz cans evaporated milk
1	tsp vanilla	1	cup chopped pecans or walnuts

In a large pan, stir together sugar, butter and corn syrup. Place over medium heat and bring to a boil. When boiling well, slowly add evaporated milk a little at a time so mixture never stops boiling. Stir constantly with a wooden spoon. Cook to 235° on candy thermometer. Add vanilla and nuts. Pour into greased pan and do not scrape pan as pouring. Takes at least 2 hours.

CHICKEN ENCHILADAS

1	chicken, cooked, boned, diced	1	can diced green chilies
2	cans cream of chicken soup	12	flour tortillas
$^1/_2$	pt sour cream		Grated cheese
1	onion, chopped		

Heat sour cream and soup. Stir in chicken, onion, diced chilies and as much grated cheese as desired. Heat until thoroughly combined. Pour some of the mixture into the bottom of an oblong 2-inch-deep pan. Put some of the mixture into each tortilla and roll them up. Place filled tortillas in pan side by side. Pour the rest of chili mixture over the tortillas. Sprinkle top with more grated cheese. Bake in 350° oven for 30 minutes.

COLD CUCUMBER-WALNUT SOUP

1	cup shelled walnuts	1	tsp salt
6	large cucumbers, peeled, seeded, and thinly chopped	$^1/_2$	cup finely chopped scallions, including green tops
2	large cloves garlic, minced		Juice of 1 lemon
1	qt buttermilk	$1^1/_2$	cups plain nonfat yogurt
$1^1/_2$	Tbs finely minced dill	$^1/_4$	tsp white pepper

Place walnuts on a cookie sheet. Roast in a preheated 350° oven for 15 to 20 minutes. When cool, rub walnuts between your palms to remove skins. Chop and set aside. Mix all other ingredients together. Put $^1/_2$ to $^2/_3$ of this mixture into a food processor and process until smooth. Return to original bowl. Add walnuts and mix well. Cover bowl and refrigerate at least 4 hours before serving. Serves 6.

CAA TRAIL RIDE

ROCKY MOUNTAIN NATIONAL PARK makes for a spectacular backyard, and Lynn and Doug Erion are fortunate to have the park surrounding their property north of Estes Park, Colorado. I heard the brand stands for Erion's place north of Estes Park.

For the 1989 trail ride, chairmen Fritz White and Herb Mignery made arrangements for us to camp on the Erion property. We enjoyed snow-splotched mountains, crystal cool mornings and rippling creeks. The ride took place inside the park along beaver-dammed creeks and across treeless plateaus overlooking Estes Park. There were no facilities for team roping so everyone pitched horseshoes. Bob Pummill and Red Steagall claimed to be camp champions. Harvey Johnson's new tent served as the campsite landmark on the trail ride map. Newest CAA member, Roy Grinnell, learned to hold his own in the give-and-take of the get-together. Mel Warren, after a two-year absence, was back on the ride, and Dave Halbach was still going through initiation. Emeritus member Frank McCarthy attended the trail ride, and during the meeting, members voted him back into active status. There were a number of painting excursions to record various sections of the Rocky Mountains.

On one rainy day, just a few of us were in camp sitting around the campfire in yellow slickers and ponchos telling stories and making light conversation. Bud Helbig was so relaxed he kept dozing off. During one particularly loud snoring period, we decided to play a joke on him. Everyone disappeared behind tents and vans, leaving poor Bud sitting there alone, sleeping in the rain. Gary Niblett was behind a tent and, looking through its windows, could see when Helbig awakened. Bud looked around casually, slowly stood up, stretched his hands out toward the warmth of the fire, and nonchalantly surveyed the camp.

By this time Niblett was bent over in laughter and Bill Owen's muffled snickers could be heard off to the left. Still Helbig searched for some sign of a yellow slicker. He turned his back to the campfire, clasped his hands behind him, and checked the other side of camp. He stretched up on his toes, still looking around. Finally, Fred Fellows laughed and walked into view, followed by Pat Haptonstall, Bill Nebeker, Niblett, Owen, Steagall and Watson. Everyone has a good laugh on Bud every time the story is retold and enlarged upon.

CAA TRAIL RIDE

COWBOY ARTISTS OF AMERICA celebrated its twenty-fifth anniversary in 1990. CAA was having its trail ride in California for the first time, and new members Roy Andersen and Jim Norton were attending their first ride.

The O'Neill family hosted the ride at the Amantes Campsite on the 40,000-acre Rancho Mission Viejo. This working cattle ranch is just five miles east of San Juan Capistrano. When we arrived, cook Bob Reed already had his chuck wagon set up

and hors d'oeuvres set out. The first morning was California-bright under a clear blue sky. By nine A.M., riders were heading out for the day's ride. To help settle the trail dust, the hosts provided a well-stocked and manned porta-bar that followed the riders out of camp. The bartender commented that he served more sodas, juices and Sharps than anything else.

Roy Grinnell practiced the art of "fanning" his mount, at the wrong time. He discovered it was much easier and safer to don his slicker while standing on the ground.

Each afternoon, at cow camp a half-mile away, there was team roping and a number of horsemanship demonstrations. In camp, there were two horseshoe pits and a raised tee for practicing golf shots. Scattered around camp were tents, vans, suburbans and an RV; two guests just spread their sleeping bags out on the ground, under the stars.

At night, around the campfire pit, Rusty Richards—formerly with the Sons of the Pioneers—Red Steagall, Herb Mignery, Bill Nebeker, John Hampton, Buck Bean, Don Hedgpeth and Bill White, who was a 1987 trail ride host in Hawaii and who also furnished some of the horses for this ride, provided guitar music and/or vocalizing. CAA Museum Director Gene Ball, played some bluegrass on his banjo, and Mehl Lawson fiddled around on his violin. Herb, by popular demand, did his Elvis impersonation. Beeler says there were reports of accordian music some time after midnight.

The fifth generation of the O'Neill family is now on Rancho Mission Viejo. The family was well represented by Gil Aguirre and Buck Bean. They even presented CAA with a trail ride flag they had designed.

EMERITUS MEMBERS

ESTOFADO

1	lb lean beef, cut into 1" cubes	1/8	tsp pepper
1	Tbs cooking oil	1	clove garlic, minced
1	cup dry red wine	1	recipe Bouquet Garni (see below)
1	cup tomatoes	1/2	cup sliced mushrooms
1	large onion, sliced thick	1/4	cup sliced ripe (pitted) olives
1	green pepper, cut into strips	1	Tbs all-purpose flour
1/4	cup raisins	1	cup cold water
1/4	cup dried apricot halves	3	cups cooked rice, hot
1	tsp salt		

Raw rice about triples when cooked;
precooked rice doubles.

BOUQUET GARNI: Tie 1 tsp each of dried basil, thyme and tarragon plus 1 bay leaf together in cheesecloth.

Brown meat in a large skillet in oil. Add the next eleven ingredients, including Bouquet Garni; simmer, covered, for 1 hour. Add mushrooms and olives and simmer 30 minutes more. Discard Bouquet Garni. Combine flour and cold water, stir into stew and cook until mixture thickens and bubbles. Be sure to stir constantly. Serve over hot rice. Serves 6.

RUM COOKIES

1	cup butter, or margarine	1	lemon rind, grated
1/4	cup sugar	1/4	cup rum, or brandy
2	cups flour	1	egg white
1/4	tsp salt		Pecan halves
3	egg yolks from hard-boiled eggs		Cinnamon & sugar for dusting

Mix first seven ingredients and roll thin. Cut into fancy shapes, brush with egg white and dust with cinnamon and sugar. Garnish with pecan halves. Bake at 375° until light brown.

"QUICKIE" SWEET PICKLES

12	large sour pickles, NOT dill	1	Tbs mustard seed
3	cups sugar	1	stick cinnamon
1	Tbs celery seed	1/2	cup raisins

Slice pickles into non-metal container. Add remaining ingredients to enough water to cover pickles. Pour over pickles. Let stand overnight. Enjoy!

PHILADELPHIA SCRAPPLE

1	qt water	$^{1}/_{2}$	tsp sage
1	cup white cornmeal	$^{1}/_{2}$	tsp thyme
1	lb pork liver sausage, crumbled or finely chopped	1	tsp salt
3	onions, diced		Pepper to taste

Bring water to boil, let boil after adding each ingredient in order; then cover and simmer for $1^{1}/_{2}$ hours, stirring frequently. Pour into loaf pan and cool. Slice and fry. If 1 pint of milk and 1 pint of water are used as the liquid, the scrapple will brown more easily. Serves 4.

TEXAS CHILI SAUCE

50	tomatoes, or 5 qts
25	onions
1	bunch celery
6	green peppers, sweet
6	red peppers, sweet
1	Tbs allspice
1	Tbs cinnamon
1	Tbs mace
1	Tbs ground cloves
1	qt vinegar
1	cup sugar
2	Tbs salt

Chili Peppers: Poblano—rather mild pepper used in chilies rellenos. Tepin and Pequin (dried)—both tiny fireballs. Two or three Tepin will season a pot of chili. Pequin are good in sauces and stews. The larger Guajillo is the most used in Mexican cooking. The Jalapeno is the all-purpose pepper, "Functional fieriness at its best."

Grind all ingredients together; boil slowly for 2 hours, stirring often to keep from burning. Store in refrigerator, or bottle in usual manner.

CAA TRAIL RIDE

IN MID-APRIL OF 1991, the members of CAA and a few guests headed for the 6666 Ranch in the Texas panhandle. It was windy, warm and dusty—typical for that time of year around Guthrie. Honorary member Red Steagall is a good friend of the folks who manage the Four Sixes, and through him, CAA had been invited to join in a few days of roundup.

The historic 6666 Ranch was started by Samuel Burk Burnett in the 1870s; he ran it until his death in 1922. Now the day-to-day operation of the ranch is handled by J. J. Gibson, with help from his wife, Naida, and son, Mike.

When we arrived, an old 6666 chuck wagon was already set up, and ranch cook Joe Propps was preparing the evening meal of beef, beans, potato salad, carrots, slaw, biscuits and cobbler. There was always iced tea and lemonade available and "Miss Naida" recommended a 50-50 mixture of the two. As usual, there was singing, music and storytelling well into the night.Wake up was at 5:30 with a breakfast of biscuits, gravy, eggs, bacon and hot coffee. By daybreak, almost everyone was saddled up and riding out. For two days the ranch hands, artists and guests gathered and worked cattle and marked and doctored calves. Many of these activities were recorded by the weekly television show "The West" for later broadcast. Everyone there was seeing some of the best stock around being handled in the old way, a privilege few of us "cowboys in our hearts" get to experience.

The artists were given a tour of the "big house," a stone mansion built in 1917, to see the art collection and early photographs of ranch, family and famous guests. Some of the CAA riders accepted an invitation to rinse off the trail dust before heading south to Kerrville for the CAA Museum anniversary.

I have finally figured out why cowboys get up so early and work so hard: they have to to keep from gaining weight on the fine food that cookies like Joe Propps and his crew produce.

OVER THE YEARS, CAA members and their guests have been very lucky to share the time, food, ranches and fellowship of some wonderful people who have invited us into their midst. Sometimes they knew little about CAA and were just taking the word of a friend that everything would be okay. No doubt a number of times the routine of the ranch was thoroughly disrupted; for this we apologize. For your cooperation, caring and sharing, we give you our sincerest thanks.

HORSE SHOE

1 cup cream sauce	1 tsp Worcestershire sauce
¹/₂ lb grated sharp cheddar cheese	¹/₄ tsp dry mustard
OR	5-6 slices bread, toasted
1 can Campbell's cheddar soup	
¹/₄ cup milk	

Combine first four ingredients and heat until well mixed. Serve 2-3 tablespoonfuls of hot sauce over any one of the following items on toast:

1. Fried bacon and sliced tomatoes. 2. Shrimp, shelled, fresh or canned. 3. Hamburger patty. 4. Turkey or chicken, sliced, with sliced tomatoes.

WITH TWO SLICES OF TOAST ON A PLATE, it's called a Horse Shoe, one slice of toast and it's a Pony. Years ago, when the Leland Hotel was open in Springfield, Illinois, this was a popular item on the menu.

A.B.C.D.
(A Beans & Cream Dish)

¹/₂ cup chopped onion	1 can sliced mushrooms, drained & sliced
¹/₂ cup chopped celery, or more	
¹/₂ cup (1 stick) butter	¹/₂ cup heavy cream
2 pkgs frozen lima beans, cooked & drained	Salt & pepper to taste

Using a large saucepan, sauté onion and celery in butter until done. Add cooked limas, and other ingredients, mix. Warm but don't boil. This is a country recipe created before the word *cholesterol* entered our vocabulary. It's the only way I like limas. Serves 10.

FRENCH PIE CRUST

3	cups flour	1	egg, beaten
1	tsp salt	5	Tbs ice water
1¼	cups shortening	1	tsp vinegar

Mix flour, salt and about two-thirds of shortening until the size of peas, use a pastry blender, then blend in remaining shortening. Dribble egg over dough. Combine water and vinegar, add to flour mixture. Gently stir and toss with fork until mixed. Has a flaky texture and handles easily. Makes three 9-inch crusts.

CHICKEN SOUFFLE

16	slices bread, remove crust & quarter	½	cup chopped green chilies
3	cups milk	1	cup chopped onion
3	eggs, beaten	1	cup chopped celery
½	cup grated sharp cheddar cheese	4	cups chicken breasts, boiled & cubed
2	cans cream mushroom soup	1	cup mayonnaise
1	tsp butter		Salt & pepper to taste

Lightly butter the insides of a large ovenproof dish, about 12-x 10-x-2 inches. Line the bottom with 8 slices of quartered bread. Combine the chopped vegetables, chicken, mayonnaise and salt & pepper and spread over bread; cover with other 8 slices of bread. Mix milk and eggs and pour over mixture. Spoon on undiluted mushroom soup. Spread out evenly and top with grated cheese. Cover and refrigerate overnight. Bake at 325° for 1 hour 15 minutes to 1 hour 30 minutes. This freezes well and is good reheated. Serves 10-12.

TAGLIONE

2	lbs ground round steak	1	*2 can* creamed corn
1	green pepper, chopped	1	*2 ½ can* tomatoes
2	cloves garlic, chopped & pressed	2	Tbs chili powder
1	large onion, chopped		Salt & pepper to taste
1	8 oz pkg wide noodles	½	cup grated sharp cheddar cheese
1	can pitted ripe olives, chopped		

Sauté meat, pepper, garlic and onion. Cook noodles. Combine all ingredients, except cheese, in a casserole. Sprinkle cheese on top. Bake at 350° for 1 hour. Serves 8-10.

*See Appendix.

SPICE CAKE SAUCE

1	cup brown sugar	1	large lump butter
2	Tbs flour	1	oz brandy, bourbon or scotch
1¼	cup boiling water		(optional)

Mix sugar and flour together in pan, add a little cold water and stir until mixed. Put lump of butter into boiling water and slowly add to the first mixture. Cook, stirring constantly, until thick. Remove from heat and add alcohol if desired. Serve immediately over squares of spice cake. This was served to my parents in Canada over forty years ago; one of Dad's favorites. Serves 4-5.

FLEMISH STEW

1	medium onion, chopped
1½	lbs stew meat, cubed
	Salt & pepper to taste
	Pinch thyme
1	can beer
	Cooking oil

Brown onion and meat in a small amount of oil. Add seasonings. Put in casserole and pour in beer. Cover and bake at 350° for 2½-3 hours. Check it at about the last hour; you may wish to reduce heat or increase the liquid. Also excellent way to cook venison. Serve over noodles or wild rice. Serves 3-4.

Fruit and cheese for dessert: the highs and lows induced by the fruit sugars can be offset by the proteins or complex carbohydrates of cheese.

Cut warm breads, cakes and pies with a hot knife.

CHILI CORN CASSEROLE

2	(8-oz) cans white kernel corn	1	8-oz pkg cream cheese
1	(4-oz) can chopped green chilies	1	stick margarine or butter

Drain corn. Melt butter and cream cheese; add corn and chilies. Mix well and pour into a greased 8-x-8-inch baking dish. Bake at 350° for 30 minutes.

FRENCH CREAM CAKE

CAKE:

1   cup sugar
3   eggs, separated & beaten
1½ cups flour
3   Tbs water
2   tsp baking powder
    Pinch salt

FILLING:

2   cups milk, heated in double
    boiler
1   cup sugar
2   eggs, well beaten
2   Tbs cornstarch, softened in a
    little cold milk
½   cup butter
    Flavoring and fruit as desired

CAKE: Add yolks to sugar; gradually beat in flour, water, baking powder and salt. Gently fold in beaten egg whites. Bake in two layer pans at 300° for 40 minutes.

FILLING: Stir sugar, eggs and cornstarch together until smooth, then stir into hot milk. Continue stirring over boiling water until mixture thickens. Remove from heat and add butter and again stir until smooth. Add desired flavoring (vanilla, almond, lemon) and cool.

FOR SERVING: Split cake layers and spread custard between them, or put fruit between some layers and custard between others, or on top.

THERE IS NO FAMILY CONSENSUS on what fruit Grandmother used. Some say bananas, some say black cherries and others say peaches. I think it was probably whatever fruit she had on hand. This was a special dessert, served when the pastor called, when one of the girls brought home a suitor, or when Grandfather came home from a journey. I hate to spoil a good story but Brownell won't touch the stuff, says it's too rich and he'd rather have an ice cream cone.

CUBAN BREAD

4   Tbs yeast
2   Tbs sugar
1   Tbs salt
    Cornmeal

2   cups water, lukewarm
6+ cups flour
    Grease

Dissolve yeast, sugar and salt in a little lukewarm water. Mix flour and remaining water into a batter. Combine the two mixtures; add enough flour to get a manageable dough. Turn out onto a floured board and knead until stiff and smooth. Place in a greased bowl, cover with a damp towel and let double in size. Turn out onto a lightly floured board. Cut in half and shape into two round loaves. Grease baking sheet, sprinkle with cornmeal and place loaves thereon. Let rise 5 minutes, cut a cross on each with a sharp knife and put into a cold oven. Place a large pan of boiling water in bottom of oven, set temperature at 400° and bake for 45 minutes.

STOLLEN

4	cakes yeast	3/4	cup chopped pecans
1	pt milk, scalded and cooled	3/4	cup chopped almonds, blanched
2 1/2	lbs flour, warmed	1	tsp salt
1 3/4	cups sugar	1/2	cup chopped walnuts
4	eggs	1	lb candied fruit, chopped (citron,
3/4	lb butter, softened		orange, lemon—NO cherries)
1	lb raisins	1	tsp cinnamon
1/2	lb currants		

Break up yeast, cover with warm water and let stand for 30 minutes. Put half the scalded milk into a warm bowl and add enough flour to make a thin batter. Add the yeast mixture to this and let stand in a warm place for about one hour, until it's thoroughly bubbly. Sift the rest of the flour into a large pan and warm it in the oven.

Combine sugar, eggs, remaining milk, butter, candied fruits and all other ingredients; add the yeast mixture. Slowly add the liquid to the flour, mixing from the top down, keep some flour on the bottom as you mix. Continue mixing until all the flour is absorbed and dough comes away from the pan. Cover the dough and let it rise in a warm place for about one hour. Divide the dough into four equal parts and knead thoroughly. Place in well-greased loaf pans and let rise again in a warm place for one hour.

Spices don't have calories so use them liberally.

Bake at 375° for fifteen minutes, then decrease heat to 325° for forty-five minutes more or until rounded and a dark golden brown. They should make a hollow sound when thumped. DO NOT underbake, they should be brown on all surfaces and firm in texture, not doughy. This is bread, not coffee-cake. It is traditionally cut on Christmas Eve and served with every meal throughout the season. Makes 4 loaves.

A DILLY OF A DIP

1	cup sour cream	1 1/2	tsp Beau Monde seasoning
1	cup mayonnaise	1 1/2	tsp minced onion
1 1/2	tsp dill		

Blend and refrigerate at least 2 hours. Great with vegetables.

GRANDMA SNIDOW'S APPLE DUMPLIN'S
(that's Sni-dough)

3	cups flour	³/₄	lb butter, more or less
1¹/₂	cups Crisco	2	tsp cinnamon
1	tsp salt	1	cup brown sugar
¹/₂	cup cold water	¹/₂	tsp cloves
6-8	apples, peeled & sliced as for pie	¹/₂	tsp nutmeg
2	cups sugar, more or less	3	Tbs flour

Mix the first four ingredients and chill. Then roll dough thin and cut into six 8-inch circles. Fill circles with 1 cup apples, 2 tablespoonfuls sugar, a dash of cinnamon and a lump of butter; hold in hand, shape into a ball and squeeze top together, place in pan. Bake at 400° for 50 minutes. Make syrup by combining 1 cup sugar, brown sugar, 2 tablespoonfuls butter, 3 tablespoonfuls flour and ¹/₂ teaspoonfuls each of cinnamon, cloves and nutmeg; bring to boil. Pour syrup over dumplings and cook 10 minutes more. Makes about 8 dumplings. Serve with ice cream.

LEMON ANGEL PIE

CRUST:

4	egg whites
1	cup sugar
¹/₂	tsp cream of tartar
1	lemon rind, grated
1	cup whipping cream

FILLING:

4	egg yolks
¹/₂	cup sugar
4	Tbs lemon juice

CRUST: Beat egg whites frothy, add cream of tartar and beat stiff; as eggs thicken, add sugar (two tablespoonfuls at a time). Pour into pie tin, one with high sides, and bake at 300° for 40 minutes. Cool.

FILLING: Beat egg yolks, add sugar, lemon juice and rind. Cook in double boiler until thick and spongy. Cool. Whip the cream and fold it into the other mixture. Pour it into the pie crust and put in refrigerator for several hours. When I spray the pie tin with Pam it makes it easier to get the pie out.

GREEN CHILI DIP

1	pint sour cream	2	8-oz cans green chilies,
	Garlic salt to taste		peeled and chopped

Mix all ingredients, cover and chill in refrigerator overnight.

GREEN CHILI STEW

1¹/₂	lbs lean pork roast, ¹/₂" cubes	1	Tbs oregano
6	cups water	1-2	Tbs red chili powder
1	cube chicken bouillon	4	cans tomatoes, drained
1	onion, chopped	2	30-oz cans
5-7	cloves garlic, chopped and pressed		diced green chilies
1	Tbs comino	4	Tbs brown sugar

Sear meat in pan, add water and bouillon cube. Simmer. Add onion, garlic, sugar and spices, mix. Add tomatoes, chilies and salt to taste and simmer for at least 4 hours. More water may be added if necessary. Two dozen fresh green chilies, roasted over charcoal, peeled and chopped may be substituted for the canned chilies. The kind of green chilies determines how hot the stew will be; they vary from mild to hot. Serve hot. Good frozen and reheated.

MOM'S RAW APPLE CAKE

1	cup oil	4	cups chopped apples
2	cups sugar	1	cup chopped pecans
1	tsp vanilla	1	tsp cinnamon
1	tsp chopped almonds	2	eggs
2	tsp soda	1	egg white
2¹/₂	cups flour	¹/₂	cup white corn syrup

Combine all ingredients except the egg white and corn syrup, mix well. Pour into cake pan and bake at 325° for 1 hour. Combine egg white and corn syrup, beat with electric mixer until it stands in peaks, add a few drops of flavoring. Spread icing on cooled cake.

BISQUICK BEER BREAD

2¹/₂	cups Bisquick	1	can beer, preferably malt
2	Tbs sugar		

Combine ingredients and mix well. Place into a greased loaf pan. Bake at 375° for 40-45 minutes to a golden brown.

DUTCH BABIES

PER PERSON:	$^1/_4$ cup milk
1 egg	$^1/_4$ stick butter, never exceed a
$^1/_4$ cup sifted flour	total of 1 stick

Place butter in a souffle dish and put into oven; set temperature at 425°. While butter is melting, put eggs into blender; blend on high. Add milk and mix well. Continue to blend and add flour, 1 tablespoon at a time; when thoroughly mixed, set blender on lowest speed so mixture won't settle. When butter has melted, remove dish from oven, careful it's hot! Swirl dish around so butter coats all sides; place dish on cooling rack. Pour mixture into center of hot dish and immediately put into oven. Bake at 425° for 20-22 minutes. Serve on warm plates with warm maple syrup.

THE ROUNDUP

PER PERSON:	ODDS & ENDS:
2 slices bacon	Cheese, longhorn
2 eggs	Green onion
1 Tbs milk	Tomatoes
Fresh ground black pepper	Green peppers or chilies
	Mushrooms

Fry bacon crisp, drain on paper towels. Slice, dice, chop and/or grate all odds and ends. Save a little bacon grease and sauté vegetables. Meanwhile, beat eggs, add milk, season to taste and mix well. Crumble bacon into cooked vegetables, add egg mixture and scramble (stir) until almost done; at the last minute add cheese, heat until melted. Use odds & ends in the combination and amounts dictated by personal taste. I use this recipe to roundup everything left in the refrigerator at the end of the week. Serve on Oven Toast.

OVEN TOAST

Bread	Butter

Place bread under broiler and toast. Remove bread, turn over and butter untoasted side. Return to oven until butter has melted and edges are brown.

BREAKFAST EGGS

6	eggs	2	slices day-old bread
2	cups milk	1	lb sausage
1	tsp salt	1	cup grated cheddar cheese
1	Tbs dry mustard		

Mix first four ingredients and beat with a fork. Cut day-old bread into cubes and place in 9-x-12-inch baking dish. Fry and drain meat; cut meat into bite size and place over bread in pan. Pour the first mixture over the bread and meat. Refrigerate overnight, 10-12 hours. Sprinkle cheese on top and bake at 350° for 45 minutes. Good for overnight guests. The next morning you can visit while breakfast is cooking. Serves 6-8.

BISCUITS

5	cups flour	2	cups buttermilk
3	tsp baking powder	1/4	cup warm water
1	tsp baking soda	1	pkg dry yeast
1	tsp salt	1	cup shortening
1/3	cup sugar	1/4	cup butter, melted

Dissolve yeast in warm water. Put all dry ingredients in large bowl, add shortening and cut in by hand. Mix dissolved yeast with buttermilk and add to dry ingredients by hand. Work the dough on a well floured board until smooth, roll out and cut biscuits. Place on a greased cookie sheet. Brush tops with melted butter, cover and place in freezer. Makes 40 +. Take out the desired number and bake at 400° until brown.

FOR PARTIES: use same ingredients but double the amount of sugar. Roll dough to $\frac{1}{4}$" thickness, cut with biscuit cutter, dip into melted butter and fold in half. Place on cookie sheet and bake in same manner. While still hot, dust with powdered sugar.

BANANA PUFFS

1	cup pancake mix	$\frac{2}{3}$ cup milk
2	Tbs brown sugar	3 Bananas
1	egg	Vegetable oil for frying
	Powdered sugar for coating	

Combine first four ingredients and mix until well blended. Peel bananas and cut into 1" pieces, dip into batter and fry, on end, in hot oil in skillet until brown. Pieces brown quickly, turn and brown other end. Remove and drain on paper towel. Sprinkle with sugar and serve hot. Serves 6-8, or less.

BROKEN HEARTS DIP

2	30-oz cans artichoke hearts, drained	1 cup Best Foods mayonnaise
		$\frac{2}{3}$ cup fresh grated Parmesan cheese

Mash artichoke hearts with a fork, combine with other ingredients and mix well. Put in ovenproof serving dish. Bake at 350° for 20 minutes. Serve with melba rounds. It will disappear so fast every one will be broken-hearted. Jean Halbach adds $\frac{1}{4}$-$\frac{1}{2}$ cup each of chopped black olives and chopped green chilies.

RED HOTS

1	lb hamburger meat	1 can Ro-Tel tomatoes & green
1	can Campbell's cheddar cheese soup	chilies, drained

Brown meat. Add cheese soup and tomatoes & chilies. Cook over low heat until well mixed. If you can't find Ro-Tel, use 4 ozs medium Picante and 4 ozs chopped green chilies; serve over toast. Serves 2-4.

QUICK DIP

1	lb Velveeta cheese, cubed	1	can Ro-tel tomatoes with green
2	Tbs instant chopped onion		chilies and cilantro

Mix Ro-tel and onion in a medium-sized bowl. Heat in microwave on high heat for two minutes, stir well. Add half the cheese and heat 4 minutes, stir well. Add remaining cheese, heat 4 minutes longer and stir well. Serve warm.

SKILLET STEAK STEW

1	lb ground round steak	2	cups tomato sauce
$^1/_4$	cup chopped onion	2	Tbs vegetable oil
1	egg	4	carrots, diced
2	tsp salt	1	cup celery, diced
$^1/_4$	cup fine bread crumbs	2	potatoes, quartered
1	Tbs Worcestershire sauce	1	cup water
$^1/_8$	tsp pepper		Oil to brown

Lightly brown meat and onions in oil. Pour off excess fat. Combine egg, 1 teaspoon salt, bread crumbs, Worcestershire, pepper and 1 cup tomato sauce. Add to meat. Stir thoroughly and cook for several minutes. Add remaining ingredients. Cover and simmer for 2 hours, stirring occasionally. Serves 4.

MEXICAN CORNBREAD

3	eggs, separated	1	cup grated longhorn cheese
2	cups cornmeal, yellow	$1^1/_4$	tsp baking soda
1	cup cream style corn, yellow	$^3/_4$	cup vegetable oil
1	cup sour cream	$^1/_2$	cup milk
1	tsp salt	$^1/_2$	cup chopped jalapeno peppers
1	tsp sugar		or 1 cup chopped green chilies
1	cup chopped onions		

Beat the egg whites stiff. Mix other ingredients and fold in the stiffly beaten egg whites. Pour into ungreased 9-x-16- or 12-x12-inch pan and bake in a preheated 350° oven for 1 hour. It's even hot when it's cold. It makes a big difference in whether you use jalapeno peppers or green chilies.

NO-ROLL PIE CRUST

1 tsp salt
1¹/₂ tsp sugar
¹/₂ cup Mazola oil

2 Tbs milk
1¹/₂ cups flour

Mix salt, sugar, oil and milk in a large bowl. Add flour and mix with fork until all flour is absorbed. Pour in middle of 10-inch pie plate, work with fingers toward rim. Even out all over plate, do not poke any holes. Pour in filling, bake as directed for filling. Good for pecan and custard pies; especially good for pumpkin pie. Not good for a pre-cooked crust.

COCKTAIL SAUSAGES

1 cup brown sugar
1 tsp dry mustard
   Toothpicks

1 cup wine vinegar
2 lbs hot sausage, rolled into
   marbles, or cubed links

Brown sausage on all sides, but do not cook too hard. Drain on paper towels. Boil all other ingredients about 10 minutes. Put sausages into a storage jar and pour the mixture over them; store in refrigerator 24 hours. Serve with toothpicks.

JERKY GRAVY

Jerky, ground or chopped fine
Flour
Milk
Little fat or grease
Salt & pepper to taste

Generally, each person will eat
1¹/₂ to 2 times as many potatoes
whipped or mashed as they
would baked.

Fry the jerky until done. Remove meat from grease, add flour to grease. Add milk, season with salt and pepper, cook. Add meat to the gravy. Serve over potatoes or biscuits. When Frank was asked how much of each ingredient should be used, he replied, "It depends on how much gravy you want."

When CAA started talking about doing a cookbook, the first recipes received were from Mary Polk.

TAMALE PIE

FILLING:

1	lb ground beef	1	tsp sugar
1	medium bell pepper, chopped	1/2	tsp salt
2	tsp chili powder	1 1/2	cups grated cheddar
1	15-oz can tamales, cut into bite-sized pieces		
1	medium onion, chopped		**CRUST:**
1	large clove garlic, chopped	2	cups cold water
1	12-oz can whole-kernel corn	1	Tbs butter
1	4-oz can ripe olives, chopped	3/4	cup yellow cornmeal
2	8-oz cans tomato sauce	1/2	tsp salt

FILLING: Slightly brown beef; add pepper, onion and garlic, sauté. Add corn, olives, tomato sauce, sugar, salt and chili powder; simmer 20 minutes, then add tamales and cheese. Pour into large casserole dish.

CRUST: Mix water, salt, butter and cornmeal; boil and stir until thick. Spread over tamale mixture. Bake at 375° for about 40 minutes or until crust is brown and done.

Frank Polk after Joe Beeler

TUNA BOATS

3	large baking potatoes, baked
2	13-oz cans of tuna, drained, save oil
1	clove garlic, minced
1	cup finely chopped celery

3	Tbs picante sauce, mild
1	Tbs chopped fresh parsley
1/2	cup grated cheese, cheddar, swiss or mozarella
	salt and pepper to taste

Cut cooled baked potatoes in half lengthwise. Scoop out and mash the centers. Sauté garlic and celery in tuna oil, add butter if necessary, season with salt and pepper. Combine everything but the parsley and cheese, mix well. Refill the potato skins with the mixture, sprinkle tops with cheese of your choice, or a mixture, and broil for 3 minutes, or until browned. Sprinkle with parsley. Serves 3-6.

Cervantes (1547-1616), Spanish writer, wrote, "There's no sauce in the world like hunger."

COWPOKE SANDWICH

1	large onion, sliced thick
	Cilantro and/or oregano, dried, crumbled
	Salt and pepper

Bread slices, buttered
Vinegar & water, equal amounts
Cayenne pepper to taste
(optional)

Put onion slices in a bowl, coat with spices, cover with water mixture; refrigerate overnight. Drain onion slices, season with salt, pepper and cayenne; place between two slices of buttered bread.

LORRAINE SCRIVER

GARBAGE BEANS

1	lb hamburger	3/4	cup brown sugar
1	jar brown beans	1/3	cup catsup
1/2	onion, diced	1/4	tsp curry powder
1/2	green pepper, diced	1/4	tsp ginger powder
1	stalk celery, diced	1/4	tsp garlic powder
1	small can crushed pineapple		Tabasco to taste, optional

Sauté meat, onion, pepper and celery until meat is no longer pink. Remove pork fat and put beans into casserole. Combine all ingredients and mix well. Bake at 350° for 1 hour. Serves 4.

BERRY SOUP

3	lbs beef ribs, with water to cover	1/2	cup sugar, or to taste
2 1/2	cups serviceberries, fresh or dried	1/4	cup flour
	(soak dry berries overnight)	1/2	cup bitterroots

Boil ribs in large pot until done, remove ribs, let broth cool and skim off fat. Strain liquid and return to pot. Add serviceberries, sugar, flour and bitterroots to make paste, simmer until bitterroots look translucent. This soup is very filling and nutritious and will stay hot for an hour without heat. Ribs may be served on the side or at a later meal. Serves 6.

Serviceberry is a small acidic fruit, green or brown, the size of a berry but actually a pome, like an apple or a pear.

S-6 SCALLOPED POTATOES

2	cups ham, diced	2	cups milk
3	large potatoes, sliced	1	Tbs mayonnaise
1	medium onion, sliced	1/2	tsp Tabasco
1	pkg cheese, grated		Paprika & parsley as desired
1	can cream of mushroom soup		

Put soup in a bowl, slowly add the milk a little at a time. Add mayonnaise and Tabasco, stir until smooth. Pour one-half of sauce into a casserole dish, then, using one-half of the items, make layers of potatoes, onions, ham and cheese. Repeat the layers in order with the remaining ingredients and pour rest of milk sauce over the top. Garnish with paprika and parsley. Bake at 350° for 1 hour or test with fork to determine doneness. Serves 4-6.

PIEGAN ASPIC

1	envelope Knox gelatin	1	bay leaf
2	cups tomato juice	1	tsp horseradish
1	Tbs grated onion juice	2	Tbs Burgundy wine
1	tsp Worcestershire sauce	$\frac{1}{4}$	tsp salt
1	tsp fresh lemon juice	$\frac{1}{4}$	tsp pepper
1	Tbs sugar	$\frac{1}{4}$	tsp Tabasco

Camel-hair brushes, often made of hair from a squirrel's tail, got their name from the inventer, Mr. Camel.

Sprinkle gelatin over 1 cup of tomato juice, set aside. Put rest of ingredients in a pot and bring to boil; let simmer for 1 minute, remove bay leaf. Stir gelatin mixture into the hot mixture and let stand until nearly set. Mix in any one or a combination of: sliced-stuffed green olives, ripe olives, and/or diced cheese, dill pickles, sweet gerkin and/or small shrimp. Chill until set. Serves 4.

BURNT-MEAT MARINADE

1	large round steak, cut into $\frac{1}{2}$" wide strips	1	Tbs lemon juice
$\frac{1}{4}$	cup Karo syrup	$\frac{1}{4}$	tsp black pepper
$\frac{1}{4}$	cup vinegar	$\frac{1}{4}$	cup Burgundy wine
2	Tbs water	$\frac{1}{4}$	tsp garlic powder
$\frac{1}{4}$	tsp Tabasco	1	tsp Worcestershire sauce
		$\frac{1}{2}$	cup Crisco oil

Mix above ingredients in glass bowl and marinate meat for at least one hour. Put meat on campfire forks or on grill and cook over glowing coals until done as desired. Good with Berry Soup and Fry Bread. Serves 4-6.

TONGUE IN BEER

3	lbs veal or beef tongue	1	lemon (for grated peel)
1	large onion, chopped	1	can of beer, warm
1/2-1	cup chopped parsley	1	pkg slivered almonds
2	cups chopped celery	1/2	cup raisins
3	Tbs butter		A pinch of cinnamon
3/4	cups sugar		Salt & pepper to taste

Cover tongue with water; add parsley, celery, onion, salt and pepper, cook for three hours. If necessary, add more water to keep tongue covered. Remove tongue from liquid. When cooled, peel tongue and cut into one-half inch cubes. Melt butter in pan, add sugar (carmalize to consistency of soft candy); add beer, grated lemon peel, cinnamon and tongue and simmer until meat is hot. Just before serving add almonds and raisins. Serve over rice. (1 1/2 to 2 cups of the tongue liquid may be saved to prepare the rice.) Serves 6-8.

SALLY SWANSON'S SAUTÉED
SHERRY SWEETBREADS WITH SPINACH

6	pairs of sweetbreads		SPINACH:
6	Tbs butter	6	lbs spinach, chopped,
1	large onion, chopped		water to cover
12	mushrooms, sliced	2/3	cup sour cream
2	cups sour cream		Salt & pepper to taste
6	ozs sherry, heated (half with rice)		Chives, pimiento and/or
1	lemon		parsley, for garnish
	Salt & pepper to taste		

Clean sweetbreads; soak sweetbreads in ice water for several hours, drain. Cover with fresh cold salted water, add the juice of one lemon, bring to a slow boil and blanch for five minutes. Drain sweetbreads and plunge into cold water. Remove and discard the tubes and membranes. Spread sweetbreads on a platter and weight them down with a plate to flatten and firm them as they cool. Melt butter, add sherry and sauté sweetbreads until lightly browned. Remove the sweetbreads and keep warm. Add onion and mushrooms to pan, and more butter if needed. Sprinkle with salt and pepper to taste and cook for about three minutes. Stir in sour cream, add sweetbreads and more sherry if necessary.

SPINACH: Heat with salt and pepper in a heavy pan over moderate heat. Drain, stir in sour cream. Place on two large platters, arrange sweetbreads on top and pour sauce over all. Can be served over rice. Serves 20.

MOUNTAIN OYSTERS

6 "oysters," bantam-egg sized, per person	Mazola oil for frying Garlic salt to taste

Clean the oysters down to their own membrane, much like a wiener. Place them on a hot griddle or skillet lightly coated with oil, sprinkle liberally with salt. Move them around until brown on all sides, they will eventually pop open, like popcorn. Serve hot.

THE WAY TO START THESE RECIPES is to raise a herd of bull calves, castrate them and feed them to preferred size. My family got the tongue recipe from artist Stiles Dickenson when he was 70 years old; I was 16. As for the "oysters," these choice morsels are thrown into the dirt at some brandings; at others, they are tossed onto the branding fire until they burst and are eaten right there. We save them.

You can see, when we butcher, we use most everything: Mountain Oysters, Sweetbreads, and Tongue.

BROWN BETTY

3 cups sliced apples	$^1/_2$ tsp nutmeg
$1^1/_2$ cups bread crumbs, soft	$^1/_4$ cup melted butter
$^1/_3$ cup brown sugar	$^3/_4$ cup warm water
1 tsp cinnamon	

Toss apples, crumbs, sugar, cinnamon and nutmeg together in a bowl. Turn into a buttered $1^1/_2$-2 quart baking dish. Combine butter and water; pour over apples. Bake at 350° for 40 minutes, or until apples are tender. Serve with hard sauce, ice cream.

KEDGEREE

3 hard-boiled eggs, chopped	1/2 tsp salt
2 cups hot cooked rice	2 Tbs melted butter
2 cups cooked flaked fish	$^1/_3$ cup cream
Dash mace or nutmeg	

Mix and cook in double boiler. Serve for breakfast (traditional) or lunch. Serves 6-8.

CHICKEN FRICASSEE

2 Tbs butter
2 Tbs oil
4 lbs chicken parts
1 onion, chopped
2 cups chicken stock
$^1/_2$ lb mushrooms, sliced
3 carrots, peeled & sliced
1 cup cream
2 egg yolks

It must have taken extreme courage or unbearable hunger to have first discovered that mountain oysters were edible.

Someone told me mountain oysters tasted like fish, so I tried them; now I can't eat fish because it tastes like mountain oysters.

Heat butter and oil in dutch oven or casserole; brown chicken on all sides over low heat. Add onion and stock, cover and simmer for 15 minutes. Add mushrooms and carrots, cover and simmer 15 minutes longer. Beat together cream and yolks. Spoon a bit of hot stock into cream, stir until smooth. Pour cream mixture over chicken. Heat slowly, do not allow to boil. Serves 4.

MUSHROOMS IN WINE

1	lb fresh mushrooms	3	Tbs chopped parsley
$\frac{1}{4}$	cup butter	3	Tbs chopped chives
6	Tbs dry white wine		Salt & pepper to taste

Slice mushrooms and sauté in butter; stir in remaining ingredients and simmer 3-5 minutes. Serves 4.

TOP SIRLOIN BARBECUE

3½-4 lbs top sirloin	⅛ tsp ground cloves
2 cloves garlic	2 Tbs wine vinegar
½ tsp black pepper	¼ cup olive oil
Dash cayenne	

Mash above ingredients well with the back of a spoon and rub into top sirloin. Place meat in a shallow bowl and splash on olive oil. Turn meat to coat all sides and cover with plastic wrap. Keep at room temperature 2 hours, turning occasionally. Start charcoal fire early (45 minutes required for the right heat). Place meat 5 inches above coals and turn often. Total cooking time is 45 minutes-1 hour.

BAKED INDIAN PUDDING

5 cups milk, scald 4 cups	1 tsp cinnamon
⅓ cup sugar	½ tsp ginger
½ cup yellow cornmeal	1 tsp salt
⅔ cup dark molasses	4 Tbs butter

To scalded milk, add sugar, cornmeal, molasses, spices, salt and butter. Cook until thickened, about 20 minutes. Put into greased baking dish. Add 1 cup cold milk, but do not stir. Bake at 300° for 3 hours. Serve warm with whipped cream, or ice cream.

NAVAJO SQUAW BREAD

2 cups flour, not sifted	½ tsp salt
4 tsp baking powder	Lard & water

Mix dry ingredients and add ½ cup warm water, not too hot. Make soft dough consistency. Work and knead out air bubbles. Slap to make flat pancake-shaped patties about 8 inches in diameter. Using skillet half full of melted lard or shortening, drop patties into very hot fat. When golden brown, drain on paper. Good cooked in one-half bacon dripping and one-half shortening.

Always face the stove so no one will talk about your cooking behind your back.

SQUASH CASSEROLE

1	cup (¹/₂ lb) butter or margarine	1	can cream of mushroom
12	oz pkg herb-seasoned dressing		or cream of chicken soup
	mix	1	cup sour cream
3	cups sliced or diced cooked	1	large onion, grated
	squash, drained (zucchini or	3	large carrots, grated
	crookneck)	¹/₄	tsp ground black pepper

Melt butter and toss with herb-seasoned dressing mix. Mix half of dressing-mixture with squash, cream soup, sour cream, onions, carrots and pepper. Turn mixture into lightly greased 13-x-9-x-2-inch baking dish and spread evenly. Sprinkle remaining dressing mixture over all. Bake in preheated 350° oven for 45-55 minutes. Serves 8.

BLACK-EYED PEA SALAD

2	cans Trappy black-eyed peas with	2	medium tomatoes, diced
	jalapenos, drained	2	avocados, diced
¹/₂	cup chopped onion	8	oz Catalina dressing
¹/₂	cup chopped celery		

Mix and let marinate overnight. Serves 6.

MEXICAN LAYERED SALAD

2	cans bean dip	1	pkg taco seasoning
3-4	ripe avocados	2	small cans chopped ripe olives
¹/₂	tsp lemon juice	2	green onions, chopped, tops
	Salt and pepper to taste		included
2	cups sour cream	3-4	medium tomatoes, chopped
1	cup grated cheddar cheese		

Layer ingredients in 8-x-8-inch serving dish in following order: 1. In bottom of dish, spread bean dip, 2. Make guacamole by mashing avocados and adding lemon juice, salt and pepper, 3. Mix sour cream and taco seasoning and layer on top of guacamole, and 4. Top with olives, onions, tomatoes and grated cheese. I make a separate layer of each. Serve with tortilla chips for dipping. A very colorful and delicious salad. Serves 10 or so.

Rhubarb is a vegetable,
the stalk of which is used as a fruit.
"They say" the leaves are poisonous.

CHEESECAKE

CRUST:
1²/₃ cups finely rolled graham
    cracker crumbs
2   Tbs sugar
1¹/₂ tsp cinnamon
6   Tbs butter, melted

FILLING:
9   ozs cream cheese
1   tsp vanilla
1   cup sugar
3   eggs

TOPPING:
1   pt sour cream
3   Tbs sugar
¹/₂ tsp vanilla

CRUST: Mix ingredients and pat into bottom and sides of deep 10-inch pan. Chill in refrigerator.

FILLING: Beat the cream cheese thoroughly, gradually add cup of sugar, add eggs one at a time continuing to mix, then add the 1 teaspoon vanilla. Pour into chilled pie shell and bake at 300° for 30 minutes, or until toothpick comes out clean.

TOPPING: Whip the sour cream and add the last two ingredients while whipping. Pour over baked pie and bake at 500° for 5 minutes. Place in refrigerator. Serve cold. Serves 6-8.

CHOCOLATE NUGGETS

1   cup semi-sweet chocolate
    chips (6 oz)
3   Tbs corn syrup
1   tsp vanilla

¹/₂ cup evaporated milk
¹/₂ cup powdered sugar
2¹/₂ cups vanilla wafer crumbs (1/2 lb)
1   cup finely chopped nut meats

Melt chocolate in large double boiler. Remove from heat and stir in corn syrup and vanilla. Gradually stir in milk, sugar, wafer crumbs and nuts, mixing after each addition. Let stand in refrigerator for about 30 minutes. Shape into one-inch balls and roll each in chocolate decorettes, shredded coconut, chopped nuts or other goodies. Chill. Makes 4¹/₂ dozen.

S.O.B. BRISKET

1   bottle Liquid Smoke
2   large onions, chopped
6   oz barbeque sauce to taste

4-6 lb brisket, whole
    Salt, garlic salt and celery salt
    Worcestershire sauce

Drizzle liquid smoke all over brisket. Liberally season with salts and cover with onion. Cover roaster and refrigerate overnight. Before cooking, pour off liquid smoke (keep it for the next brisket) and douse the brisket with Worcestershire sauce. Cover and bake at 275° for 5 hours. Uncover, pour on barbeque sauce and bake one hour more. Great for other roasts too. Serves 6-8.

GRITS CASSEROLE

1 cup grits	$\frac{1}{4}$ cup milk
3 cups water	1 4-oz can chopped green chilies
Velveeta cheese to taste	$\frac{1}{4}$ cup sharp cheese, grated
$\frac{1}{4}$ cup (4 tbs) margarine	Salt & white pepper to taste
2 eggs, well beaten	Paprika, dash

Cook grits according to directions on box, except use 3 cups of water instead of 4. When grits are done, add remaining ingredients, except paprika and sharp cheese. We like it real cheesy so I add as much Velveeta as possible. Pour into greased baking dish and bake at 300° for 45 minutes. Remove from oven, top with grated sharp cheese and paprika. Return to oven and bake for 15 minutes more. This is a terrific do-ahead dish and stays hot for pot luck dinners and picnics. Serves 8-10.

Poaching eggs: use a small saucepan and milk instead of water. Place the poached egg on toast, pour the warm milk over it, salt and pepper to taste.

ONE DAY IN 1970, Jim was finishing a watercolor that had gone extremely well and he was especially pleased with the result. My day had not gone well. Suddenly I realized it was nearly dinner time and not only was nothing ready, I didn't even have anything in mind. I went into the studio, walked up behind Jim's chair and stood there a couple of minutes, still thinking about dinner. Jim was sitting there anticipating an enthusiastic response to his painting and the praise he thought I was about to shower upon him. Instead, I asked, "Will hamburgers be okay for dinner?" Jim recovered barely in time to reply, "Yeah, they're okay," as I'd already turned and was headed out the door. It wasn't until years later, when Jim was telling the story to a large group, that I realized the other side of the story. Jim has told the story many times since. He says that whenever he is feeling particularly smug about a painting, he recalls this incident; it is his equalizer. Since then I have tried to be more sensitive to other peoples' feelings, remembering, "Man does not live by bread alone!"

PUMPKIN CHIFFON PIE

1	9-inch pie crust	1	tsp cinnamon
1/3	cup brown sugar	1/2	tsp allspice
1/3	cup finely chopped pecans	1/2	tsp ginger
2	eggs, separated	1/4	tsp cloves
1	can (1 lb) pumpkin	1 2/3	cups (13 ozs) evaporated milk or
3/4	cup sugar		light cream
1/2	tsp salt		

Place crust in pie pan, flute around edge. Sprinkle brown sugar and pecans into bottom of shell. Beat the egg whites until stiff, set aside. Beat yolks, add remaining ingredients and mix well. Gently fold whites into the mixture and pour into pie shell. Bake in preheated 425° oven for 15 minutes, reduce heat to 350° and bake 45 minutes more, until inserted knife blade comes out clean. Cool and serve with whipped cream. Serves 6-8.

*Unbroken raw egg yolks
dropped in cold water
will keep for several days.*

KAHLUA CHOCOLATE CAKE

1	pkg Betty Crocker yellow cake mix	1	cup Kahlua
1	pkg instant chocolate pudding	1/4	cup vodka
1	cup oil	3/4	cup water
4	eggs	1/2	cup powdered sugar

Combine first seven ingredients and mix with electric beater for four minutes. Pour into a greased 9-inch tube cake pan. Bake in a preheated 350° oven for 50 minutes. Cool for 30 minutes. Glaze with a mixture of powdered sugar and enough Kahlua to make desired consistency. I got this recipe from Diane Skor, wife of frame-maker Walter Skor.

MUSHROOM AND ONION QUICHE

1	lb mushrooms, sliced thin	4	eggs
1	lb white onions, chopped	1	Tbs flour
2	Tbs butter	1/2	tsp salt
1	9-inch pie crust	2	cups cream

Sauté mushrooms and onions in butter until transparent. Place pie crust in a pan. Arrange mushrooms and onions in pie shell. Beat the other ingredients together and pour over the mushrooms and onions in the shell. Bake at 375° for about 45 minutes, until puffed and brown. Serve warm. Serves 4-6.

BANNOCK
(Camp Bread)

6	cups flour	2	tsp salt
7	tsp baking soda		Water

Build an open campfire and let it burn down to glowing coals. Mix dry ingredients with enough water to make dough manageable by hand. Lightly grease a cast-iron skillet, not too much grease or the dough will fry. Put a chunk of dough into the pan. Make a fist and shape the dough into a round cake about 1/2-inch thick. Poke a hole in the center with your finger; the hole will allow the heat to penetrate and bake evenly, like a donut. Use a rock or small log to prop the pan up facing the hot coals. As the bread begins to brown, twist the pan sideways so all areas will cook and brown evenly. When the first side has browned sufficiently, flip the bread over and cook the other side until browned and done. Remove from pan and pass around. Everyone breaks some off as it is passed. Serve hot with butter, jelly, jam or syrup. Eat it with breakfast. Makes 6 six-inch cakes, equal to about 18 biscuits. I got this recipe from my father, he got it from his father. Father used to mix up the dough in the top of the flour sack.

POT ROAST OF BEEF

2¹/₂-3 lbs pot roast	2-3 stalks celery, coarsely chopped
2 Tbs flour	2 Tbs chopped green pepper
1¹/₂ tsp salt	1 clove garlic, minced
1/4 tsp pepper	1 bay leaf
2 Tbs cooking oil	¹/₂ cup beef broth or bouillon, warm
1 large onion, coarsely chopped	2 Tbs minute tapioca, optional

Mix the flour and salt, dredge the meat in it, covering all sides. Add oil to large skillet and brown the meat on all sides, add more oil as needed. Mix onion, celery, pepper and garlic. Place about ²/₃ of this mixture into the bottom of a 3¹/₂-quart crock pot. Put in the bay leaf and meat. Add the rest of the vegetable mixture. Then pour the broth, or bouillon, over the meat. Cook on high for 1 hour, reduce heat to low and cook for 5-6 hours more, until meat is tender. Remove bay leaf. Slow cooking results in a lot of liquid, so if you like the gravy thicker, add the tapioca. Serve the meat sliced, with some of the gravy over it. Serves 6.

Red meat should be browned
quickly, uncovered.

Steaks should be turned once only
while being cooked.

IN VANCOUVER, BRITISH COLUMBIA, John always ate lunch at a little restaurant across the street from where he worked. He always ordered his favorite dish. After a time, as soon as the waitress saw him walk through the door, she would sing out this order, "Pot Roast of Beef and nothing to drink." That was in 1925. Sixty years later, John still ordered "Pot Roast of Beef."

CHICKEN CORDY CACCIATORE

- 1 fryer chicken, cut up
- 1 24-oz can tomato sauce
- 1 12-oz can stewed tomatoes
- 1 large green bell pepper,
    cut into strips, optional
- 1 clove garlic
- 1 tsp butter
- 1 bay leaf
- 1 onion, chopped
- 1 small can tomato paste
- 1 tube anchovy paste
- 1 Tbs oil
- 1 tsp oregano
- Parmesan cheese
- Pepper to taste
- No salt

Sauté garlic in oil and butter until golden; discard garlic. Brown chicken, set aside. Sauté onion and pepper; add all other ingredients, including chicken, except cheese. Cover and simmer on low for 1 1/2 hours, or until meat is tender. A can of rolled anchovies with capers adds more flavor, but must be blended with a bit of tomato sauce, in blender, before being combined with other ingredients. Serve over spaghetti, sprinkle with parmesan.

ROBERT
LOUGHEED

BOB'S BARBEQUED BURGERS

2 lbs hamburger, lean chuck	2 eggs
5 slices shredded bread	2 tsp Grey Poupon mustard
2 Tbs ketchup	5 Tbs barbeque sauce, or to taste
1 cup chopped scallions, greens too	Chopped onions, to taste
Teriyaki to taste	

Combine ingredients; mix thoroughly. Make patties; cook on grill.

OHMYGOSH GOULASH

FILLING:

1 lb hamburger
$^1/_2$ lb mushrooms, sliced
1 green pepper, chopped
1 medium onion, chopped
1 can (16 oz) whole or stewed
   tomatoes

$^1/_2$ Tbs oregano
Garlic powder, salt and pepper
   to taste

TOPPING:

$^1/_4$ cup sour cream
Dill weed to taste

Brown hamburger, drain off grease. Add mushrooms, green pepper and onion, sauté 5 minutes. Add tomatoes and spices; cover and simmer 20-30 minutes. Serve in soup bowl, add a dollop of sour cream on top and sprinkle with dill weed. Good served with garlic bread. Serves 4.

B B CASSEROLE
(Beef & Bean)

1	lb ground beef	2	tsp brown sugar
1/4	cup diced green pepper	2	tsp vinegar
1/2	cup diced onion	1	tsp mustard
1/2	cup diced celery		Salt & pepper to taste
1/2	cup water	1	#2 can* pork & beans
1	cup (8 ozs) tomato soup		

Combine all ingredients, except pork & beans, and sauté until vegetables are soft. Put pork & beans in casserole dish, pour the hot mixture on top and bake at 375° for 45 minutes. Serves 8.

*See Appendix.

135

CHILIGHETTO

1	lb ground beef	2	cups tomato juice
2	tsp fat	1	tsp Worcestershire sauce
1	onion, chopped	1/2	tsp pepper
1	tsp chili powder	1 1/2	cups raw spaghetti
	Salt to taste	2	cups kidney beans

Brown beef in fat, add onion, chili powder and salt; cook until onion is tender. Pour into casserole. Combine other ingredients, mix well, pour over meat. Cover and bake at 350° for 1 hour. Serves 6-8.

HOMEMADE TOMATO SOUP

3	medium tomatoes, peeled, cored, chopped	3	Tbs butter
1	small onion, finely chopped	3	Tbs flour
1/4	cup chopped celery	1	tsp salt
1/4	tsp sugar		Pepper to taste
3	whole cloves	3	cups milk, warmed
1	small bay leaf		Water

Combine first six ingredients in water to cover. Bring to boil, reduce heat and simmer for 15 minutes, set aside. In large saucepan melt butter, stir in flour, salt and pepper, cook for one minute. Add warmed milk to butter mixture and cook until thickened, stirring often. Remove the bay leaf and cloves from tomato mixture. Puree in blender and gradually stir into the milk. Reheat. Serves 6. Freezes well.

You'll make good marks with your family

When sautéing or frying, always heat the pan first and then add the oil or butter.

Cowboy Life   Geo Phippen ℰ℘

FRIED POTATOES WITH ONIONS

3-4 slices bacon   1   small onion, chopped
4-5 medium potatoes, peeled   Salt & pepper to taste

Fry bacon in skillet over medium heat. Meanwhile, slice potatoes in uneven slices; they
don't stick together as much. When bacon is almost done, add potatoes. Increase heat so
potatoes will brown; turn to brown both sides. When potatoes are almost done, add onion.
Cover the skillet the last few minutes to steam the potatoes done. Try half a cup of diced
okra in lieu of onion, but add it to the bacon so it will brown.

FRIED LIVER AND ONIONS

2-3 slices bacon
    Liver, cut into 1/2" slices
1   medium onion, sliced

$\frac{1}{4}$ cup flour, more if needed
  Salt & pepper to taste

Onions will keep longer if you wrap them individually in aluminum foil.

Fry bacon over medium heat until crisp. Meanwhile, place liver slices on paper towels to absorb excess juices. Remove bacon from pan. Put flour, salt and pepper into a paper bag; drop liver slices, one or two at a time, into flour and shake bag to coat liver with flour. Put floured slices into skillet with bacon grease, over medium heat, and cook until crisp and brown. Turn and brown second side, don't over-cook. Separate onion slices into rings and fry with liver the last few minutes of cooking time. Crumble crisp bacon over top of liver on serving platter.

GEORGE ALWAYS LOVED A GOOD STEAK in addition to the above dishes. He also enjoyed cooking outside, but wasn't known to be the greatest. One time on a picnic, George was showing his sons how to make baking powder biscuits in a dutch oven. They came out a nice golden brown. While we were eating, our dog came up to the table and started begging. George gave him one of the biscuits. The dog took it, immediately dug a hole and buried the biscuit. We never let George forget it.

BROCCOLI CHEESE SOUP

2 Tbs salad oil, or margarine	³/₄ cup chopped onion
6 cups water	8 ozs fine egg noodles
1 tsp salt	2 10-oz pkgs chopped broccoli
¹/₈ tsp garlic powder	6 cups milk
1¹/₂ lbs American cheese, chopped	6 bouillon cubes

Heat oil and sauté onions for 3 minutes. Add water and bouillon cubes, heat to boiling, stirring occasionally. Add noodles, a few at a time; cook 3 minutes. Stir in broccoli and garlic powder, cook 4 minutes more. Add milk and cheese, cook until cheese is melted.

CHOCOLATE BREAD PUDDING

2 cups scalded milk	1 cup bread pieces
¹/₄ cup sugar	2 Tbs cocoa
1 egg, slightly beaten	1 tsp vanilla
1 lump butter	Pinch of salt

Dissolve cocoa in milk. When milk is slightly cooled, add bread. Pour rest of ingredients into milk, mix. Pour into buttered baking dish. Bake at 350° for 45 minutes. Serves 4. Don't wolf it down, enjoy it. If desired, serve with Vanilla Sauce.

VANILLA SAUCE

1 lump butter	$^1/_3$ cup sugar
$^1/_2$ tsp vanilla	$^3/_4$ Tbs flour
$^3/_4$ cup water	Pinch of salt

In small saucepan, combine sugar, flour and salt. Gradually add water. Stir until smooth. Simmer over low to medium heat, stirring constantly, until thickened. Remove from heat. Stir in butter and vanilla.

SALMON LOAF

1 cup cracker crumbs	$^1/_2$ cup chopped onion
1 can celery soup	$^1/_4$ cup chopped green pepper
$^1/_3$ cup mayonnaise	1 Tbs lemon juice
1 egg, beaten	1 large can red salmon, drained

Mix above and bake in greased loaf pan at 350° for 1 hour. Serves 4.

BALD-FACED SANDWICH

1	lb Velveeta cheese, cubed	3-4	Tbs milk
1½	lb bacon, fried crisp, 1" pieces	4	Tbs Miracle Whip
6-7	tomatoes, ripe, peeled, chopped	4	ribs celery, chopped
6	slices toast, buttered		Salt & pepper to taste

Drain tomatoes. Mix bacon, Miracle Whip, tomatoes and celery; season to taste. Combine milk and cheese in sauce pan and melt over low heat. Place a slice of toast on a plate, cover with tomato mixture, top with cheese sauce and serve. Makes 6.

CHICKEN BUNDLES

7½	ozs thinly sliced ham	3	ozs white wine, or 2 ozs lemon juice
6	slices cheese, swiss or jalapeno		Soy sauce, ground pepper,
3	slices liverwurst		hot sauce, chopped onion,
6	chicken breast halves, boned and skinned, save skins		etc., to taste
	Butter, softened		

Separate ham slices, lay out 5 slices, one at a time, each overlapping one-half of the previous slice. Put slice of cheese on first ham slice and place half slice of liverwurst on cheese; roll everything together. Pound chicken breast halves flat. Roll ham bundle inside a flattened breast half; wrap all in a piece of skin. Repeat until all the meat is used. Place bundles into a casserole dish and brush each with butter. Pour wine over meat; top off with a dash or two of soy sauce and ground pepper to taste. Bake at 325° for 45 minutes. Bundles may be tied with string and charcoaled on grill. Serves 3-6.

COW-CHIP COOKIES

1/2 cup butter	1/2 cup shortening
1 cup sugar	1 cup brown sugar, packed
1 cup flour	1 cup whole wheat flour
2 cups oats	1 tsp baking soda
2 eggs	1 tsp baking powder
1/2 tsp salt	1 pkg (12 ounces) semi-sweet
1 tsp vanilla	chocolate chips

Cream butter, shortening, vanilla and two sugars, stir in eggs. Add flours, salt, baking soda and powder; mix well. Add oats and chips; mix. Form on cookie sheet by plopping down large spoonfuls 4-5 inches apart. Bake at 350° for 10-12 minutes. Makes 18.

MUSHROOM & GARLIC BREAD

1 loaf French bread	1 can mushroom pieces
1 stick butter or margarine	Garlic salt to taste

Cut bread diagonally in 3/4-1-inch-thick slices; butter each slice. Drain mushrooms and pat dry on towel; place mushroom pieces on buttered bread. Sprinkle with garlic salt. Place slices on cookie sheet and toast under broiler to desired browness. Serve with spaghetti and pesto sauce.

PESTO SAUCE

2 cups fresh basil leaves, packed	2 cloves garlic
2-3 tsp pine nuts	salt to taste
1/2-3/4 cup grated romano/parmesan cheese	1/2 cup olive oil

Put all dry ingredients in food processor and blend. Slowly add oil and continue to blend. Serve on spaghetti. Serves 4.

MA'S DRESSING

Fresh fruit of the season, cleaned
and cut to bite-size
$^1/_2$ cup sugar
2 Tbs flour
1 egg, beaten

1 Tbs butter
2 cups liquid (small can frozen
orange juice plus fruit juices)
1 lemon, juice & rind
$^1/_2$ Tbs celery seed

Mix sugar and flour; add fruit juices and cook until thickened. Remove from heat and, while stirring, add egg, small amount at a time. Return to heat and cook one minute more. Remove from heat and add celery seeds, butter, lemon juice and rind. Serve over fresh fruit.

CHUCK WAGON CHOCOLATE CAKE

2 cups sugar
$^1/_3$ cup cocoa
4 eggs, separated
2 cups flour, sifted
1 tsp vanilla

1 cup butter
$^1/_2$ cup water, hot
$^1/_2$ cup water, cold
1 Tbs baking powder

Cream the sugar and butter; mix the cocoa and hot water, combine the two mixtures. Add yolks, mix well. Add flour, mix thoroughly. Add cold water, vanilla and baking powder, mix. Beat whites until stiffened, fold whites into other mixture. Bake at 350° about 25 minutes.

LINE SHACK SALAD

8-10 potatoes, boiled, skinned,
sliced
1-2 onions, diced
$^1/_4$ lb bacon, cut into 1" pieces

2-3 Tbs flour
$^1/_3$ cup vinegar
$^2/_3$ cup water
Sugar to taste

Fry the bacon, when almost done add $^1/_2$ of the onions and continue to cook until tender. Meanwhile combine the cooked potatoes and the other $^1/_2$ of the onions, set aside. When the bacon is cooked, add the flour as if making gravy, stir. Combine the vinegar and water and slowly add it to the gravy mixture, stirring constantly. If the mixture gets too thick, add more water, but never more vinegar. Add sugar to taste. Pour the hot mixture over the potatoes and onions, mix well. Serve warm.

SKINNY DIP

2 cups low fat cottage cheese, drained	1 cup chopped green onion tops
4 tsp dill	2 tsp milk

Mix all ingredients and blend in blender until smooth. Chill. Serve with assorted bite-sized vegetables on toothpicks.

PEANUT BUTTER PIE (COLD)

2 qt vanilla ice cream	1 cup ($^1/_2$ pint) whipping cream
1$^1/_2$ cups peanut butter	3 9-inch graham cracker pie shells

Blend the ice cream, cream and peanut butter. Fill the three pie shells and freeze. Optional: sprinkle a few graham cracker crumbs or peanut halves on top of each pie.

PEANUT BUTTER PIE (HOT)

1 cup corn syrup
1 cup sugar
$^1/_2$ tsp vanilla
3 eggs, slightly beaten
$^3/_4$ cup creamy peanut butter
1 unbaked pie shell

Generally, each person will eat 1$^1/_2$ to 2 times as many eggs scrambled as they would fried.

Blend the first five ingredients. Fill the pie shell. Bake in a preheated oven: 400° for 15 minutes; then 350° for 30 minutes.

CRUNCHY CHICKEN

10-12	chicken breast halves, boned	1	clove garlic, pressed
2	cups Ritz cracker crumbs	2	tsp salt
3/4	cup grated parmesan cheese	1/8	tsp pepper
1/4	cup snipped parsley	1	cup (2 sticks) melted butter

Preheat oven to 350°. Mix crumbs, cheese, parsley, garlic, salt and pepper. Dip each piece of chicken in butter and then shake in dry ingredients (I use a plastic bag). Coat well. Arrange meat in shallow open casserole. Pour remaining butter over all. Bake at 350° for 1 hour. DO NOT TURN!! Good hot, or cold for a picnic. Serves 6-8.

MEXICAN CHICKEN CASSEROLE

8	chicken breast halves, cooked until tender, skinned, boned, cut bite size	2	cans (8 oz) chopped green chilies
		2	cups grated longhorn cheese
1	onion, chopped	1/2	cup sour cream
1	clove garlic, pressed		Picante sauce (optional)
2	Tbs oil	1	tsp coriander
1	can (14 1/2 ozs) tomatoes, hand-mashed	1	tsp salt
		1 1/2	dozen corn tortillas
		1	can cream of mushroom soup

Sauté onion and garlic in oil until tender. Add tomatoes, chilies, soup, cream, picante sauce, coriander and salt. Stir as you heat well. Add 1 cup of grated cheese and stir until melted. Cut 9 tortillas in quarters and place in bottom of an oiled casserole dish. Place one-half of the chicken on top of tortillas and then one-half of the cheese sauce. Repeat with rest of tortillas, chicken and sauce. Sprinkle remaining cup of cheese on top. Bake uncovered at 325° for about 45 minutes. Serves 6-8.

PETITE PIZZAS

1	lb cheddar cheese, grated	1	4-oz can chopped green chilies, without seeds
1	bunch green onions, chopped		
1	small can ripe olives, chopped	8	English muffins, broken in half
1	8-oz can tomato sauce		

Mix first five ingredients well. Spread on lightly toasted English Muffin halves. Place under broiler and broil until slightly brown and bubbly. You can use topping on bread rounds for hors d'oeuvres. Or spread the muffin halves and freeze them on a cookie sheet, then store in a plastic bag. These are very good for Saturday lunch, with a salad, or for Sunday supper. Makes 16.

SPINACH DIP

1 pkg chopped, frozen spinach	¹/₂ cup Hellman's mayonnaise
¹/₂ cup green onions	¹/₂ tsp salt
1 cup minced parsley	1 Tbs medium-grind black pepper

Defrost and drain spinach; squeeze with paper towel to get out all moisture. Add other ingredients; mix and refrigerate. If you like you can sprinkle crisp bacon bits on top. Serve as spread for rye rounds or Triskits. I got this recipe from Mary Jean Weaver.

John

BEEF STROGANOFF

2 lbs fillet of beef, cut in thin strips	3 Tbs butter
Salt & pepper or Chef's Salt	2 cloves garlic, pressed
1 Tbs flour	3 Tbs grated carrot
2 Tbs butter	1/2 lb fresh mushrooms, washed, sliced
2 cups beef stock	
3 Tbs heavy sour cream	1/2 lb fresh mushrooms, washed, whole
2 Tbs tomato sauce	
3 Tbs grated onion	1 tsp instant coffee

Season beef. Blend flour with 2 Tbs butter in saucepan over low heat until "roux" bubbles and is smooth. Gradually stir in beef stock and cook over low heat until mixture begins to thicken. Boil for about 2 minutes and strain through fine sieve into a large saucepan. Add sour cream alternately with tomato paste, stirring constantly. Simmer sauce gently without boiling. Sauté the beef in a skillet with remaining butter, grated onions, garlic and carrots. When meat is brown and tender, add the beef to the sauce and taste for seasonings. Add mushrooms and simmer for 5 minutes; add coffee. Cover and simmer gently for about 20 minutes or until meat is very tender. Serve over boiled rice. Serves 4-6.

SPOON BREAD

1 1/2 cups water	1 cup milk
1 tsp salt	4 egg yolks, well beaten
1 cup cornmeal	4 egg whites, beaten stiff
2 Tbs butter	

Boil water and salt; gradually stir in cornmeal. When smooth add butter, milk and egg yolks; mix well. Fold in stiff whites. Pour into greased baking dish and bake at 350° for 30 minutes, or until firm. Serve with large lump of butter, or with gravy, or as a base for creamed chicken. Serves 4.

To separate two eggs doesn't mean to move one of them to the left and the other to the right.

THE 06's FLAT
Red Steagall and Frank Polk

I woke up drunk in the Jack County jail
My throat felt like I's breathin' fire
The sheriff gave me the option to stay 90 days
Or get on my pony and ride.

Bein' one who's accustomed to lonesome and free
Bein' jailed's not a thot I'd abide
So in less than a heartbeat I saddled my hoss
And boy how this cowboy did ride.

I hear out in Alpine they don't pay no mind
To a cowboy who drifts into town
It seemed like I'd ridden to the far side of hell
But there's lots of action around.

The air is clean as any I've seen
The water runs clear and it's good
The women are pretty and the horses are fast
But the wind pumps the water and the cows cut the wood.

I found me a maiden one Saturday nite
Who needed a ring on her hand
I took her to my camp on the 06's flat
And proceeded to make her a hand.

The winter was cold and young love was strong
I stayed pretty close to the camp
But spring came around I rode into town
And whiskey took me by the hand.

She said I ain't happy when a man ain't around
I wouldn't stay here if I could
Everything in this country either sticks, bites, or stings
And the wind pumps the water and the cows cut the wood.

When the whiskey wore off my young love was gone
I trailed her to old San Antone
I made her a promise to clean up my ways
If only she'd follow me home.

30 years later I'm still lookin' back
Thankin' God that I made the right trade
Cause the 06's flat is a fine place to live
And the greatest folks God ever made.

The air is as clean as any I've seen
The water runs clean and it's good
The women are pretty and the horses are fast
And the wind pumps the water and the cows cut the wood.

CHILIES RELLENOS

12	roasted & peeled California green chilies	1	tsp garlic salt
1/2	lb Monterey Jack cheese	1/2	cup milk
1/2	cup cornmeal	1	tsp salt
1/2	cup flour	1	egg
2	Tbs onion flakes		Oil for frying

Cut as small a slit as possible in one side of each chili to remove the seeds. Leave stem on. Pat chiles dry with paper towels. Cut cheese into 12 sticks about 1/2-inch thick and 3 inches long. Put one stick into each chili, use more cheese if chiles are large. Overlap chili around cheese stick and place in waxed-paper-lined oblong pan. After all chiles are stuffed and in pan, refrigerate for at least 1 hour. After chiles are cold and firm, put oil in skillet, and combine all other ingredients into a batter. Gently dip each chili into batter, holding one end by the stem in one hand and supporting the other end with a fork or rubber spatula. Transfer immediately into hot oil, fry until golden brown, turn once. Drain on paper towel. Serve hot. Serves 4-6.

TEXAS CHEESECAKE DELIGHT

CRUST:

1 1/2	cup flour	2	Tbs powdered sugar
1 1/2	sticks margarine	3/4	cup chopped pecans

FILLING:

LAYER 1:

1	8-oz pkg cream cheese
1	cup powdered sugar
2	cups Cool Whip

LAYER 2:

1	large box instant vanilla pudding

LAYER 3:

1	large box instant chocolate pudding

TOP LAYER:

1	large carton Cool Whip, 2 cups used in layer 1
24	maraschino cherries, with stems
3/4	cup chopped pecans
1	Hershey bar, shaved

CRUST: Combine flour, margarine and powdered sugar; mix with electric mixer until dough forms a ball. Roll out and press onto bottom of 9-x-13-inch baking dish; press pecans into dough. Bake at 350° until golden; cool.

LAYER 1: Whip cream cheese with powdered sugar; fold in Cool Whip. Spread mixture evenly over cooled crust. Place in refrigerator to set.

LAYER 2: Mix pudding according to instructions. Pour evenly over layer 1. Return to refrigerator to set.

LAYER 3: Mix pudding according to instructions. Pour evenly over layer 2. Return to refrigerator to set.

TOP LAYER: Spread Cool Whip evenly over layer 3; garnish with pecans and chocolate. Place cherries in rows about $1^1/_2$ inches apart with stems up. Keep in refrigerator until ready to serve. Serves 12.

GREEN CHILI RICE CASSEROLE

1	cup uncooked rice	1	lb Monterey Jack cheese, grated
2	cups (16 oz) sour cream	1	cup cheddar cheese, grated
1	cup chopped green chiles		Salt to taste

Cook rice according to package instructions. Combine rice, chiles, salt and sour cream, mix well. In a buttered casserole dish spread a layer of half the rice mixture, then a layer of half the Jack cheese. Use the rest of the rice mixture for the next layer and the rest of the Jack cheese to top that. Finish off the top with a layer of cheddar cheese for garnish and color. If you wish, sprinkle with paprika. Bake at 350° for 40 minutes, or until bubbly. Serves 8.

ICED TEA: try orange slices
instead of lemon.
HOT TEA: try cucumber slices,
or a dash of rum

BRIE SOUP

1	medium onion, diced	$1^1/_2$	cups julienne carrots
$1^1/_2$	cups sliced mushrooms	$^1/_2$	cup butter
1	cup white wine	5	cups heavy cream
1	lb Velveeta cheese	$4^1/_2$	ozs very ripe brie
$^1/_4$	cup sherry		White pepper & cayenne to taste
	Cornstarch to thicken		

Sauté carrot, onions and mushrooms in butter until tender, add wine and cook over medium heat for 10 minutes. Work cheeses with fork, moistening with sherry; add to vegetables and cook over low heat for 2 minutes, stirring constantly. Add pepper and cayenne to taste; add cream and heat to boil. If you use cornstarch to thicken, mix it with a small amount of water and add it while mixture is boiling. You could cook the moisture out of vegetables, add wine and puree in blender and use as thickener.

SPINACH CASSEROLE

3 pkgs frozen chopped spinach	1 stick margarine, cut up
1 can mushroom soup	1 can sliced water chestnuts
1¹/₂ rolls jalapeno cheese, cut up	1 can artichoke hearts, quartered
Seasoned bread crumbs	

Cook spinach 5 minutes and drain. Add margarine, soup, chestnuts and cheese; mix and pour into buttered casserole dish. Space artichoke pieces evenly over the top; sprinkle with bread crumbs. Bake at 350° for 25 minutes, or until heated completely.

SWEET AND SOUR SHRIMP

2 lbs fresh shrimp, cleaned	1 *2 can* pineapple chunks
¹/₄ cup sugar	¹/₄ cup vinegar
2¹/₂ Tbs cornstarch	3 Tbs butter
1 green pepper, thin strips	2 Tbs slivered ginger
1 Tbs soy sauce	Salt to taste

Melt butter in sauce pan, add shrimp and cook 5 minutes. Add other ingredients, except cornstarch, and cook 2 minutes. Mix cornstarch in a little liquid to make a paste; pour into shrimp and cook until thick. Cool slowly. Serve over rice.

PECAN PIE

1 stick butter	1¹/₂ cups sugar
1 cup dark Karo	1 tsp vanilla
5 eggs	2 cups toasted pecans
2 pie shells, unbaked	

Combine butter, sugar, syrup and vanilla; cook over low heat until butter is melted, cool. Add eggs one at a time, beating after each addition. Cover the bottom of each pie shell with one cup of pecans; pour mixture over pecans. Bake at 325° for 1 hour.

COKE SALAD

1 large pkg blackberry jello	1 cup crushed pineapple
1 12-oz Coca-Cola	1 cup black bing cherries, pitted
1 lb cream cheese	

Heat juices from fruit, dissolve jello, add cream cheese and melt. Add Coke and fruit; chill.

*See Appendix.

PRESCRIPTION
Happiness Capsules

FOR: You Good People   DATE: Now   ADDRESS: Everywhere

- 1   touch of blue sky, or stars
- 1   bit of sunshine, or moonlight
- 2   parts friendliness (it always takes more than one)
- 1   generous portion of time

Mix and warm around any radiant mesquite fire or coals. Makes hundreds of capsules.

SIG. Take one or more capsules before, with or after any recipe in this book. Refill as needed and continue medication.

John W. Reagan

John W. Reagan, M.D.

RUM CHIFFON PIE

1	crumb crust	2	cups whipping cream
6	egg yolks	1	envelope plain gelatin
1	cup sugar	¹/₄	cup cold water
¹/₃	cup rum	2	Tbs boiling water

Beat yolks until light, add sugar and beat well. Add rum and mix. Soak gelatin in cold water for 5 minutes. Add the 2 tablespoons boiling water. Reheat over boiling water until dissolved. Combine the two mixtures and cool. Whip the cream and fold in. Fill pie crust and chill.

POPPY SEED DRESSING

³/₄	cup sugar	¹/₃	cup honey
1	tsp dry mustard	1	Tbs onion juice
1	tsp paprika	1	Tbs lemon juice
1	tsp poppy seeds	5	Tbs vinegar
¹/₄	tsp salt	1	cup Wesson oil

Combine all ingredients, except oil, in blender; blend well. While blending, pour in oil very slowly. Chill for at least 2 hours before using. Especially good on Coke Salad.

COCINERO
West Texas Range Cook

CAMP BREAD

Several lbs flour	1 tsp baking soda
1 cup buttermilk, or canned milk	The ends of your fingers full of
1 tsp salt	lard, or shortening

Pour the flour into a dishpan, make a hollow. Add the other ingredients, in order. Gradually mix in flour until it forms a soft ball. Pat the ball out in a Dutch oven. With coals beneath and on the lid, cook to a golden brown. Serves 3-8. "If you make it thin, people eat a lot, but make it thick and they can't eat so much."

PAN DULCE
(Sweet Bread)

Follow the above recipe, but sprinkle sugar, cinnamon and butter over the patted dough just before you put the lid on the Dutch oven.

PSOLE

1 gal hominy	Red chili powder to taste
2 tsp oregano	

Combine all ingredients in a Dutch oven and heat well over coals.

MENUDO

10 lbs tripe, cut into small pieces	2 tsp garlic salt
	Water to cover

Combine ingredients in enamel pan and boil until soft. Drain water. Put cooked tripe and Psole (above recipe) into Dutch oven and reheat. Serves 18 cowboys. I believe in "Menudo for the Crudo," meaning its good for a hangover. So I often serve it at breakfast.

CHEF
Hyatt Regency Hotel Cook

STUFFED QUAIL

8	quail, or 6 rock hens, boned except for wings, legs and thighs		Sage to taste
1½	lbs sausage, Jimmy Dean regular	8	strips of bacon
4	oz walnuts, chopped	24	pickled quail eggs

Combine the sausage, walnuts and sage, place in refrigerator overnight. Divide this mixture into as many equal parts as you have birds; roll into balls. Stuff each bird with one of the balls and reshape the bird; wrap each bird with bacon, place each quail in a two inch ceramic cup. Bake, legs up, at 325° for 15-20 minutes, or until brown. Serve on a bed of wild rice. Cover bird and rice with perigourdine sauce. Garnish with quail eggs. If you use rock hens, use 12 strips of bacon, 2 per bird. Bake at 350° for 20-30 minutes. Quail serves 4. Rock Hens serve 6.

PERIGOURDINE SAUCE

¼-½	oz each (dry weight): shallot, rosemary, thyme and marjoram	1	oz truffles, chopped
4	oz burgandy wine	1	oz goose liver pate
4	cups brown sauce	4-6	ozs brandy, optional
		2-3	Tbs butter

Gravy too white?
Stir in a few spoonfuls of
brewed coffee

Sauté shallot, rosemary, thyme and marjoram in butter until tender. Stir constantly. Remove from heat, add wine and brandy, return to heat and reduce liquid by one-half. Add brown sauce (demi-glace), return to heat and reduce until the sauce coats a spoon, do not boil. Just before removing from the heat, mix in truffles and pate. Dried truffles should be soaked in the refrigerator overnight.

APPENDIX

Approximate Substitutes

Suppose you need item "A," but don't have it. Try substituting item "B."

"A"	"B"
1 sq chocolate	sub. 2 Tbs cocoa
1 part honey	sub. 2 parts sugar
1 part cornstarch	sub. 2 parts flour
1 Tbs cornstarch	sub. 1 egg (thickens the same)
1 Tbs cornstarch	sub. 1 Tbs quick-cooking tapioca (thickens the same)
1 egg	sub. $\frac{1}{2}$ tsp baking powder
1 egg	sub. 2 egg yolks
1 egg	sub. 2 egg whites plus 2 Tbs non-fat dry milk
1 egg	sub. 2 Tbs snow (so they say)
1 tsp baking powder	sub. 2 eggs
1 cup corn syrup	sub. 1 cup sugar plus 2 cups water, boil down 50%
1 cup brown sugar	sub. 2 oz molasses plus 7 oz sugar
1 cup wine	sub. 1 cup grape juice, same color
1 oz alcohol (booze)	sub. 1 oz strong coffee, lemon juice or wine vinegar
1 cup sour cream	sub. 1 cup milk plus 1 tsp white vinegar plus 1 scant tsp soda
1 cup sour milk	sub. 1 cup sweet milk plus 1 tsp baking powder
1 cup buttermilk	sub. 1 cup milk plus 2 tsp white vinegar, or lemon juice (let stand until it curdles--about 5 minutes)
1 cup cake flour	sub. 1 cup sifted all-purpose flour minus 2 Tbs
1 part pastry flour	sub. 40% cake flour plus 60% all-purpose flour
1 scallion	sub. 1 green onion, rub white end with cut edge of garlic clove
1 cup bread crumbs	sub. 1 cup dry flaked cereal crumbs (for crispness and flavor, cracker crumbs are a POOR substitute)
1 oz cooking chocolate	sub. $\frac{1}{4}$ cup cocoa plus 1 Tbs oil

WEIGHTS AND MEASURES
(and abbreviations)

All measurements, especially liquid ones, should be level measurements.

15 drops	equal	1	saltspoonful
4 saltspoonfuls	equal	1	teaspoon (tsp)
1 heaping tsp	equals	2	level tsp
3 tsp	equal	1	tablespoon (Tbs)
1 heaping Tbs	equals	2	level Tbs
1 cube	equals	8	tablespoonfuls
2 Tbs	equal	1	ounce (oz)
1 lump	equals	3	tablespoonfuls
4 oz	equal	1	gill (gl)
2 gl	equal	1	cup (cup)
1 cup	equals	8	ozs
2 cups	equal	1	pint (pt)
1 pt	equals	1	pound (lb)
2 pt	equal	1	quart (qt)
4 qt	equal	1	gallon (gal)
2 gal	equal	1	peck (pk)
4 pk	equal	1	bushel (bu)
1 bu	equals	64	lb

In this book, there shouldn't be much call for a bushel or a peck

#1 can	equals	$1\frac{1}{2}$ cups	equals	12 ozs
#2 can	equals	$2\frac{1}{2}$ cups	equals	20 ozs
#$2\frac{1}{2}$ can	equals	$3\frac{1}{2}$ cups	equals	28 ozs
#3 can	equals	4 cups	equals	32 ozs
#10 can	equals	13 cups	equals	104 ozs

OVEN TEMPERATURES

Slow	250° - 300°
Moderate	325° - 350°
Medium	375° - 400°
Hot or Quick	425° - 450°
Very Hot	475° - 500°

INDEX

CONTRIBUTORS

CHEF
Finney, Stephen Patrick, 155

COCINERO
Hartnett, Ramon, 154

MEMBERS:

ACTIVE
Andersen, Roy & Louann, 87
Beeler, Joe & Sharon, 2
Carter, Gary & Marlys, 52
Fellows, Fred & Deborah, 22
Grinnell, Roy & Peggy, 82
Halbach, David & Jean, 70
Hampton, John W., 8
Haptonstall, Pat & Sue, 78
Helbig, E . E. "Bud", 30
Johnson, Harvey W. & Ilse, 10
Lawson, Mehl & Barbara, 58
McCarthy, Frank, 36
Mignery, Herb & Sherry, 66
Moyers, William & Neva, 18
Nebeker, Bill & Merry, 44
Niblett, Gary & Monika, 40
Norton, Jim & Pam, 90
Owen, Bill & Mary Margaret, 32
Pummill, Robert & Shirley, 62
Riley, Kenneth & Marcyne, 56
Speed, Grant & Sue, 14
Swanson, Ray & Beverly, 74
Terpning, Howard & Marlies, 48
White, Fritz & Ina, 26

EMERITUS
Lovell, Tom, 96
McGrew, R. Brownell & Ann, 103
Polk, Frank, 113
Ryan, Tom & Jacquie, 100
Scriver, Bob & Lorraine, 117
Snidow, Gordon & Sue, 106
Swanson, Jack N. & Sally, 119
Teague, Donald, 121
Warren, Melvin & Lucille, 110

HONORARY
Justin, John & Jane, 146
Reagan, John & Elizabeth, 152
Steagall, Red & Gail, 150
Watson, Tom & Toni, 142

WIDOWS
Boren, Mary Ellen, 127
Clymer, Doris, 130
Harman, Lola, 125
Lougheed, Cordy, 133
Marks, Jo C., 135
Phippen, Louise, 137
Wolfe, Marion, 139

RECIPES

APETIZERS, DIPS
Arizona Ham Balls, 74
Bean Dip, 58
Brokenhearts Dip, 111
Cheese Appetizer, 26
Cocktail Sausages, 113
Curried Mayonnaise Dip, 82